www.wadsworth.com

www.wadsworth.com is the World Wide Web site for Wadsworth and is your direct source to dozens of online resources.

At *www.wadsworth.com* you can find out about supplements, demonstration software, and student resources. You can also send email to many of our authors and preview new publications and exciting new technologies.

www.wadsworth.com
Changing the way the world learns®

New Capitalists

Law, Politics, and Identity Surrounding Casino Gaming on Native American Land

Eve Darian-Smith
University of California, Santa Barbara

 Case Studies on Contemporary Social Issues: John A. Young, Series Editor

Australia • Canada • Mexico • Singapore • Spain
United Kingdom • United States

Anthropology Editor: *Lin Marshall*
Assistant Editor: *Analie Barnett*
Editorial Assistant: *Kelly McMahon*
Marketing Manager: *Diane Wenckebach*
Project Manager, Editorial Production: *Rita Jaramillo*
Print/Media Buyer: *Rebecca Cross*
Permissions Editor: *Kiely Sexton*

Production Service: *Mary E. Deeg, Buuji, Inc.*
Copy Editor: *Linda Ireland, Buuji, Inc.*
Cover Designer: *Rob Hugel*
Cover Image: *Eve Darian-Smith*
Text and Cover Printer: *Webcom*
Compositor: *Buuji, Inc.*

The logo for the Contemporary Social Issues series is based on the image of a social group interacting around a central axis, referring both back to a tribal circle and forward to a technological society's network.

Printed in Canada
3 4 5 6 7 07 06 05

For more information about our products,
contact us at:
Thomson Learning Academic Resource Center
1-800-423-0563

For permission to use material from this text,
contact us by:
Phone: 1-800-730-2214   **Fax:** 1-800-730-2215
Web: http://www.thomsonrights.com

Library of Congress Control Number: 2003106335

ISBN 0-534-61308-X

Wadsworth/Thomson Learning
10 Davis Drive
Belmont, CA 94002-3098
USA

Asia
Thomson Learning
5 Shenton Way #01-01
UIC Building
Singapore 068808

Australia/New Zealand
Thomson Learning
102 Dodds Street
Southbank, Victoria 3006
Australia

Canada
Nelson
1120 Birchmount Road
Toronto, Ontario M1K 5G4
Canada

Europe/Middle East/Africa
Thomson Learning
High Holborn House
50/51 Bedford Row
London WC1R 4LR
United Kingdom

Latin America
Thomson Learning
Seneca, 53
Colonia Polanco
11560 Mexico D.F.
Mexico

Spain/Portugal
Paraninfo
Calle/Magallanes, 25
28015 Madrid, Spain

To Ellie and Sam

Power, not time, separates people of different cultures.

> Dara Culhane, *The Pleasure of the Crown: Anthropology, Law and First Nations* (British Columbia: Talon, 1998, p. 43)

As a society we like to maintain the image of the noble savage, removed from his homeland, but persevering, keeping up the old ways in a modern society. We don't, though, seem to want them too close to us or let them in on the economic game.

> Eldon Shiffman, resident of Santa Barbara County, *Santa Barbara News-Press* (June 16, 2002)

Despite the usual American claim that difference is to be embraced, we aren't actually very comfortable with those who are different. We don't like to look too closely, preferring soothing images of picturesque people in charming costumes inhabiting photogenic landscapes and practicing exotic but non-threatening rituals. When another culture's practices challenge our notion of the way the world should work, we either moralize or turn away. The very natural response prevents us from really engaging with people whose lives and beliefs are at odds with our own; even worse, it allows us to retain our own mistaken, if comforting belief, that people in other cultures differ from us only in superficial aspects of clothing, color, and custom, but not in their hearts and minds.

> Charles Lindholm, anthropologist, *Los Angeles Times* (December 16, 2002)

Contents

Foreword   ix

Preface   xi

Introduction   1
Aim of the Book   2
The Indian Gaming Debates   6
Indian Gaming in California   9
A Note on Language and Definitions   13

Chapter 1   Enduring Western Stereotypes of Native Americans   15
Historical Myths and Navigating the Future   15
An Inevitable Historical Tragedy?   16
Indians as a Figment of the White Man's Imagination   17
First Contact and Impact   19
Early Colonists and Their Shifting Attitudes toward Native Americans   20
The Civilizing Process of Massacres and Missions   21
Frontier Expansion and Wild West Shows   24
Hollywood and Contemporary Stereotypes of Indigenous Peoples   30
Indian Gaming and Its Unsettling Impact Today   34

Chapter 2   Law and the Management of Indigenous Peoples   36
Introduction   36
Thinking about Law as a Mechanism of Power   38
Colonialism in the 19th Century and the Reservation Era   39
General Allotment Act (1887)   41
Indian Reorganization Act (1936)   44
The State of California and Its Treatment of Indian Populations   45
The Bureau of Indian Affairs Today   45
Jurisdiction and Sovereignty in Indian Country   47
Indian Gaming and the Continuing Issue of Legal Sovereignty   49

Chapter 3   The History of Indian Gaming in the United States   52
Introduction   52
Gaming in Las Vegas and Other Non-Indian Casinos   53
What Is Indian Gaming?   56
History of Indian Casinos in the United States   59
History of Indian Gaming in California and Propositions 5 and 1A   61
The "New Buffalo" and the Future of Native American Independence   64
Challenging the Constitution, Redefining the Law   66

Chapter 4   The Chumash Indian Casino Expansion Project   70

Introduction   70
A Brief History of the Chumash Indians   71
Missions and Slavery   73
The Chumash Band of Mission Indians Today   74
The Santa Ynez Valley   76
The Chumash Casino and Current Plans for Its Expansion   79
Local Responses to the Chumash Casino Expansion Plans   81
Positive Responses to the Chumash Casino   82
The Question of Compensation—"County Wants Slice
    of Indian Gambling Pie"   85
Negative Responses to the Chumash Casino   88
Concluding Comments   93

Chapter 5   Rich Indians, New Capitalists   95

Introduction   95
Capitalism and the Decline of the Welfare State   97
Rich Indians Are Not Real Indians   98
Are Rich Indians Good Capitalists? Doing Business
    on and off Reservations   102
Where Is "Indian Country"? Native Americans in Mainstream Politics   105

Chapter 6   Local Implications, Global Connections   107

Global Indigenous Movements   110
Global, National, and Local Connections   113

**Appendix A: Answers to Common Questions
                about Indian Gaming   115**

**Appendix B: Internet Resources on Native Americans
                and Tribal Gaming   118**

Bibliography   121

Index   127

Series Foreword

ABOUT THE SERIES

These case studies feature the work of anthropologists who address contemporary issues affecting everyday life. Each case study examines an issue of socially recognized importance in a geographical, historical, and cultural context—and provides a comparative analysis highlighting its global connections and implications. The authors write absorbing narratives that include descriptions of how they apply their skills and carry out their responsibilities in the communities and organizations they study. Their engagement with people goes beyond mere observation and research, as they illustrate from personal experience how their work has implications for advocacy, community action, and policy formation. They demonstrate how anthropological investigations can build our knowledge of human society and at the same time contribute to achieving practical objectives in the pursuit of social justice.

ABOUT THE AUTHOR

Eve Darian-Smith practiced law in Australia before obtaining her master's degree (Harvard) and Ph.D degree (University of Chicago) in cultural anthropology. She has numerous publications including *Bridging Divides: The Channel Tunnel and English Legal Identity in the New Europe,* which won the Law and Society Association's Herbert Jacob Book Prize. She also has coedited a volume with Peter Fitzpatrick called *Laws of the Postcolonial.* She is currently in the Law and Society Program at the University of California, Santa Barbara.

ABOUT THE CASE STUDY

New Capitalists explores the emerging identity of Native Americans as "rich Indians" who no longer fit the dominant stereotype of marginal peoples placed on reservations, physically and socially isolated from mainstream society. The author shows how the success of casino gaming has brought legal, political, economic, and cultural tensions with surrounding communities. Sovereign tribal groups present a distinct set of cultural values and interpretations of social justice that stand in opposition to accumulating wealth for its own sake, thereby defining their own brand of capitalism. Proceeds from gaming on reservations have contributed to improved housing, health care, education, cultural preservation, and self-esteem for native peoples. In addition, tribal leaders' increasing engagement in a wider arena of business and politics challenges outside perceptions of what it means to be Native American.

The book concludes with information on similar developments related to restoring land rights and entrepreneurial strengthening of indigenous sovereignty in Canada and Australia.

John A. Young
Series Editor
Department of Anthropology
Oregon State University
jyoung@oregonstate.edu

Preface

I wrote this book on Indian gaming precisely because I wanted to discuss the social and political significance of Indian gaming with my students, and no book existed that could help me. A few academic texts on Native American casinos have been written, but these are primarily aimed at specialists. What I wanted was an accessible and succinct book that placed the issue of gaming on reservations in a historical context and forced students to think critically about their own assumptions about how Native Americans should look, act, and behave in the 21st century.

In my classroom discussions about casinos on Native American reservations, I have found that many students respond with resentment and antagonism to the idea that Native Americans can be rich and successful business entrepreneurs. When I question students about their responses, they often are incapable of articulating why they feel the way they do. Nevertheless, they seem to be certain that it is somehow "wrong" for indigenous peoples to make money, drive SUVs, wear business suits, send their children to expensive schools, and (in their opinion as opposed to reality) be granted legal exceptions to operate outside the law of the United States. Many of these students also believe that "rich Indians" can no longer be authentic Indians, and that participating in capitalist ventures will diminish their cultural uniqueness.

Such classroom discussions motivated me to write this book, which examines basic questions such as: Why must Native Americans continue to be depicted as poor and peripheral to modern society in order to be "real" Indians? What dominant cultural attitudes lead us to refuse to accept Native Americans as being equal to white Americans? Why do we assume that Native Americans are not capable of being savvy business operators? And why do we as a society hold double standards, whereby many people consider it immoral for Native Americans to make money from gambling, but not so for people such as Donald Trump and other big business entrepreneurs?

The image of "rich Indians" is powerful and provocative. It challenges prevailing mainstream attitudes that have existed since colonial times, and which assume the inferiority of Native Americans, placing them out of sight and of out mind on distant reservations. This case study explores the image of "rich Indians" and why Indian gaming has become so controversial in the United States. While many contemporary problems confront Native American peoples today, such as legal battles over hunting and fishing rights, none of these compare to the controversies surrounding Indian gaming. This is because casinos on reservations have allowed some tribes to make significant financial profits. The result is that for the first time in this country's history, Native Americans are participating in corporate capitalism, becoming involved in party politics, and forcing the American public to take their demands and needs seriously. In short, financial profits have bought some Native Americans political, legal, and social power; and this power questions in profound ways the manner in which many non-Indians define North American citizens, society, and processes of capitalism.

Cultural anthropologists usually study minority and indigenous peoples in far-away exotic places. However, this study typifies a new direction in the discipline, to study one's own culture and focus on issues of power, politics, and identity among mainstream society as well as those who continue to be marginalized within it. Studying those in positions of authority (often referred to as "studying up") is necessary in order to examine dominant attitudes, behaviors, and the taken-for-granted assumptions that affect us all. Studying up is also necessary in order to understand the processes of globalization whereby those in positions of authority and power have a large say in how peoples across the world interact at international, national, state, and local levels. This case study, which examines one set of current issues facing indigenous peoples in the United States, touches upon all these levels and underscores the significance of cultural anthropology for understanding the complex world we live in today.

ACKNOWLEDGMENTS

There are many people to thank for helping me with this book. First and most importantly, I would like to thank the many people who generously spent time talking with me about their attitudes toward and experiences with Indian gaming. Without these people, this book could not have been written. I also warmly thank the six undergraduate students in the Law and Society Program at the University of California, Santa Barbara, who helped me conduct interviews in Santa Barbara County: Gavin Charlston, Deedra Edgar, Andrea Lindemann, Jennifer Long, Adrian Ramos, and Christina Richards shared my enthusiasm about the unfolding events in our own county. Similarly, I enthusiastically thank my colleagues in the Law and Society Program at the University of California and all those who participated in our weekly seminar series for their many constructive comments. People who generously spent time reading all or parts of the manuscript include Hillary Berk, Lisa Hajjar, Elvin Hatch, Tom Hilbink, Kathleen Moore, SpearIt, Stuart Streichler, Jenna Reinbold, and Jeanne Umana. I also sincerely thank Kate Spilde and Deron Marquez for their insights on gaming, and Shelly Lowenkopf for his very helpful editorial comments.

The research for this book was enhanced by comments from people who heard me speak on the subject of Indian gaming at the following venues: Law and Society Association annual meeting in Chicago, 1999; Geography and International Studies, University of Washington, Seattle, 2000; Faculty of Law, University of British Columbia, 2001; and the Department of Jurisprudence and Political Thought, Amherst College, 2001. For their specific comments, I thank John Young, Lin Marshall, Austin Sarat, Wes Pue, Peter Fitzpatrick, Jeffrey Sallaz, Susan Gooding, Alexandra Harmon, and the anonymous reviewers of my article "Savage Capitalists: Law and Politics Surrounding Indian Casino Operations in California," *Law, Politics and Society* (2002), Vol. 26:109–140.

With regard to the telephone survey I conducted interviewing more than 700 respondents in Santa Barbara County about the Chumash Casino expansion project in September 2002, I sincerely thank Paolo Gardinali and Raymond Wong, codirectors of the Survey Center, University of California, Santa Barbara. I also thank Michael Bourgeois for his enormous help with statistical analysis of the survey data.

Lastly, I thank my husband, Philip McCarty, for his discerning insight on Indian gaming issues, skill in graphics and computer technology, and untold patience, love, and support.

This research has been generously supported by grants awarded in 2001 and 2002 by the Institute for Social, Behavioral, and Economic Research, University of California, Santa Barbara.

INTRODUCTION

It was a steamy and wet late summer afternoon, so I grabbed my umbrella before stepping outside. I'd spent the afternoon in the cozy basement of a wonderful old four-storied brownstone building situated opposite the Library of Congress in Washington, DC, apparently built and owned by its first librarian in the early part of the 19th century. Now owned and run by the National Indian Gaming Association, the building is the headquarters for national issues about gambling on Native American reservations. I had spent some hours talking with Kate Spilde, then Director of Research for the Association. Kate's job was to organize an archive of legislation, histories, impact studies, and general media releases about Indian gaming in the United States. In the basement of the brownstone building, Kate had gathered a wonderful collection of documents to which she'd generously allowed me access. Talking animatedly about what she had achieved, Kate told me about the significance of Indian gaming and why it marked a huge step forward in recognizing the importance of Native Americans and their significance in mainstream politics. Long ignored by politicians, Native Americans have become a "hot" issue precisely because some tribes are involved in casino operations, and these operations have gained them new economic and cultural independence. Tribes involved in casino activities are a new source of potential campaign contributions, and so are actively courted by politicians.

The National Indian Gaming Association (NIGA) was founded in 1985 as a non-profit organization of 168 tribes, Indian Nations, and other nonvoting associate members. Its mission, according to one of its brochures, is "to protect and preserve the general welfare of tribes striving for self-sufficiency through gaming enterprises in Indian country." In addition, NIGA works to advance the life of Indian people and "seeks to maintain and protect Indian sovereign governmental authority in Indian Country." NIGA's brownstone building, situated in the heartland of U.S. political activity, within view of Capitol Hill and opposite the Library of Congress, represents a milestone in Native American and U.S. federal history. NIGA's office building, purchased by a tribal collective, is the very first structure of any sort to be owned by Native Americans in Washington, DC. It is only recently, thanks to money received through casino operations on Native American lands, that Native Americans have been able to buy a site for their headquarters on casino issues and establish a significant presence at the center of U.S. political action.

Stepping out of NIGA's brownstone office, Kate and I headed to a local bar for an after-work drink. Popping into one of the numerous trendy small pubs and restaurants lining the streets surrounding the Library of Congress and "the Hill," I gazed around at the crowd of well-dressed young men and women. Everyone seemed to be talking very fast, waving their hands around, and looking constantly about in an effort to catch the eye of other friends and wave to acquaintances. Kate told me this kind of frenetic activity was quite normal for the city. As I sipped my beer, I noted that almost all of the people around me were white. Certainly there was no evidence of obvious ethnic difference among the well-heeled and privileged wannabe politicians, lawyers, analysts, economists, and bureaucrats. I found the sight amusing and interesting but felt completely out of my league. To me, this was a whole new world of strange symbols, language, behaviors, and priorities. The bar scene, and in fact the whole environment of the Capitol, raised many questions in my mind, given we had just left the brownstone building and NIGA headquarters: How did Native Americans fit into this environment? What did they feel when navigating within this particular world of politics and politicians? And what did the people surrounding me in the bar and all the white middle-class colleagues they stand for think about Native Americans' newly established political presence and financial clout? Have casino operations on reservations won Indians respect and credibility? Do politicians and policy makers now take them seriously rather than dismiss them as in the past? Is the majority of the population generous in their support for Native Americans or threatened by their demand for a voice in mainstream politics and society? In short, what is the general response by Washington bureaucrats and typical middle-class Anglo-Americans to what many have called, often inappropriately, "rich Indians"?

AIM OF THE BOOK

This book is a study about casino operations on Native American reservations and the impact of so-called rich Indians on mainstream U.S. culture and politics (see Figure I.1). As a cultural anthropologist and former lawyer, I am fascinated by the range of attitudes toward the involvement of some tribes in gaming, both within Native American communities and within the wider U.S. population. This interest stems from my own upbringing in Australia, my long-term concern with Australian Aboriginal land rights, and the painful process of reconciliation that has engaged the country's national politics, particularly over the past two decades. As a lawyer, I moved to the United States in 1990 to study cultural anthropology and specifically the subfield called legal anthropology. Very simply, legal anthropology is an examination of law and legal processes in various cultural contexts, be these in different countries or within one country (see Darian-Smith 2003). The study of indigenous land rights and native peoples' fight for sovereign independence represents one exciting and politically charged arena of legal anthropology where questions of competing legal values and cultural norms are raised, and the idea of legal pluralism becomes an imperative.

Typically, cultural anthropologists study minority and marginal groups within a society at home or overseas. More and more contemporary anthropologists are study-

THE FAMILY CIRCUS   **By Bil Keane**

"... And I'll be an Indian. With a casino."

Figure I.1 Family Circus cartoon, April 20, 2002. © Bil Keane, Inc.
Reprinted with special permission of King Features Syndicate.

ing what is going on within their own societies, and then turning the scientific gaze back on those in positions of power and superiority. Until very recently, leaders in power have rarely been explored or scrutinized. The typical anthropological relationship of "us" (typically in positions of superiority and authority) examining "them" (typically minorities, "primitive peoples," and those on a lower rung of the socioeconomic scale) is being turned upside down. This process of scrutinizing those in positions of power is called "studying up" and is a new direction in cultural anthropology that has emerged over the past 20 years.

The case study examined in this book continues the trend to "study up" by exploring dominant and popular attitudes held by many in the United States toward indigenous communities living within the country's borders. These attitudes are intricately tied to the ongoing and constantly shifting political and social relations between different groups that historically fall on either side of the divide between colonized and colonizers. The emergence of Indian gaming since the mid-1980s has dramatically altered relations of power between these two loosely defined groupings of people, and in turn has affected dominant cultural attitudes toward Native Americans in both positive and negative ways.

Studying Western attitudes about non-Western peoples presents only one side of the coin. The other side is how Native Americans have viewed, and continue to view, the dominant white population—a theme that I touch upon only tangentially in my chapter discussions (see Jacobs-Huey 2002). Fortunately, more and more books are being written that detail the histories of the Indian perspective, by both native and non-native Americans (for wonderful examples see James Wilson (2000) *The Earth Shall Weep: A History of Native America;* Ronald Wright (1992) *Stolen Continents: The Americas through Indian Eyes Since 1492;* and Devon Mihesuah (1998) *Natives and Academics*). These studies are important and give a more balanced view of past events as well as contemporary issues, such as Indian gaming, that continue to be infused with enduring colonial attitudes.

Cultural anthropologists question society's basic assumptions and attitudes that are largely taken for granted by most of us who constitute the dominant perspective. They seek to bring a critical perspective to contemporary issues, and their questions help us to reflect upon why we think and act the way we do—behavior that is often unconscious. For instance, I conducted, with the help of a crew of telephone operators, a phone survey of over 700 Santa Barbara County residents in September 2002 to ascertain local attitudes toward the expansion of a nearby Indian casino. This survey data allowed me to collect information from many more people than I could ever hope to personally interview, and so was useful to gauge general community thoughts and reactions. However, the downfall of a phone survey is that the information collected is necessarily superficial. First, you can ask only the set questions specified in the survey, and so you do not have the capacity or time to let the people being interviewed add their own independent thoughts. Second, as an interviewer, you get no clues from facial expression, body language, or the setting in which the interview takes place—all important ingredients when conducting a face-to-face conversation. Third, and most importantly, survey questions usually cannot get at the unconscious and taken-for-granted assumptions that people hold. These deeply held beliefs are often hard to articulate, and usually appear, if at all, in roundabout ways through face-to-face conversations and observation of behaviors displayed over long periods of time.

Anthropological research, in contrast to a survey, seeks to go beyond the obvious data collected in this mass format. So while anthropological research is often supplemented by survey data, it is not equivalent to survey generalizations. Anthropological research helps us recognize and understand prevailing attitudes and stereotypes about people who differ from the cultural majority, and who may on first appearance not fit in if they hold different values, ideas, religions, behaviors, languages, and styles of living. By scratching below the surface, anthropologists try to force people to confront their attitudes about others and ask why we think others who are different from ourselves should act and behave in certain ways.

In the past, many anthropologists were determined to show through their comparative research how white European culture and people were superior in contrast to those who were generally classified as "primitive" and "uncivilized" natives. Today, however, such colonial attitudes of superiority and inferiority are no longer acceptable, or even the main goal of cultural anthropologists. The central purpose of current anthropologists is to help us all be better future citizens by making us recognize that our own individual views are not necessarily the best or the most appropriate for all those who share our social, political, and economic worlds. Appreciating that a particular view is only one of many possibilities is essential for a fuller understanding of how people live together, and through diversity create new ways of thinking about and acting in the world. As Wendy Rose, a Native American, states, "All of us, native and non-native, are ethnocentric at our deepest levels. No amount of anthropological training or insight can abolish ethnocentrism, although we can become aware of it and learn to take it into consideration on a day-to-day basis" (Rose 1992:410).

How many people reading this book can claim to be Native American, or consider a Native American person a friend or member of the family? Why should we care about how indigenous peoples fare in this country? This book explains why understanding majority attitudes toward Native Americans is vital for a better understanding of our beliefs and assumptions about others in society. It is also necessary in order for us to appreciate the interrelationship of social, political, and economic organizations and structural systems that perpetuate stereotypes and discriminatory practices. These benefits have ramifications for everyone living and working in the United States regardless of ethnic background or color of skin. We all have a responsibility and duty to understand ongoing cultural, political, and economic discriminations, despite the relatively small population of Native Americans in this country, which according to the latest census statistics is about 2.4 million, less than 1 percent of the total U.S. population.[1]

A dominant society often projects onto minority "others" its collective fears and concerns. The general sense among many people living in the United States today is that the capitalist-driven pace of living is too fast, that we are consumed by materialist values, and that notions of community and family are being compromised in the process. In contrast, the historical image of Native American peoples is that they live quite literally in another world, untouched and unblemished by capitalist morals, deeply connected to land and nature, and upholding family and community relationships as central to their communal lifestyle. Native Americans often represent an idealized and romanticized vision of a past era, and a model of social relations no longer available or accessible to a majority of people. So it is important for the dominant non-Indian North American population to retain a belief that some resemblance of "authentic" Indians still exist, which in turn bolsters a hope, although false, that a golden past could possibly be returned to one day. In short, projecting onto Native Americans a "backward" and "nonmodern" lifestyle is vital to help non-Indians feel better about themselves and their future in a turbulent and fast-changing world. The price of this projection, however, is that it helps sustain false ideas about Native peoples and locks into place shallow stereotypes and cultural understandings about them that provide the breeding ground for intolerance, stigmatization, and discrimination.

In this context, it is helpful to remember the words of Felix S. Cohen who wrote *The Handbook of Federal Indian Law* in 1942 and was one of the most distinguished proponents of legal reform relating to Native Americans throughout the 1930s and 1940s:

> The issue we face is not merely of whether Indians will regain their independence of spirit. Our interest in Indian self-government today is not the interest of sentimentalists or antiquarians. We have a vital concern with Indian self-government because the Indian is to America what the Jew was to the Russian Czars and Hitler's Germany. For us, the Indian tribe is the miners' canary and when it flutters and droops we know that the poison gases of intolerance threaten all other minorities in our land. And who of us is not a member of some minority? (Cohen 1949, cited in Josephy et al. 1999:73)

---

[1]"Resident Population Estimates of the United States by Sex, Race, and Hispanic Origin. April 1, 1990 to July 1, 1999, with Short-Term Projection to 1 September, 2000." (http://www.census.gov).

It is important for us to appreciate how this country has historically treated its indigenous peoples. We need to examine the way popular media represents contemporary Native American cultures and societies, and why our legal and political system continues to discriminate against this minority group. How Americans, of whatever cultural background or ethnicity, treat native peoples says a great deal about our social attitudes, expectations, and future visions for a more just and democratic society. Understanding the place of Native North Americans in mainstream society, and recognizing why many non-Indians continue to hold certain prejudicial and biased attitudes toward them, is vital if we are ever to change and build a better world.

THE INDIAN GAMING DEBATES

This book could have been about many issues currently facing Native Americans in the United States, such as the legal battles over fishing and whaling rights facing the Inuit peoples in Alaska, or water rights demanded by tribes such as the Wind River Indian reservation in Wyoming, or the use of reservations as toxic dumps for nuclear waste now confronting tribes such as the Skull Valley Goshutes in Utah, or the continuing poverty and unemployment facing many Native Americans across the country. All these tribes and their legal issues are important and make up the wider social, economic, political, and legal context in which Indian gaming debates must be situated. However, I focus specifically on the issue of Indian gaming precisely because (a) it is a recent phenomenon that has emerged only since the 1980s and so is not bowed down with long-standing historical debate and legal interpretation; (b) casino operations are the only means to-date whereby some Native peoples can make significant profits and claim a right to be involved in mainstream politics and society; and (c) no other activity presents so many cultural conflicts and mass understandings between Indian and non-Indian populations. In short, the issue of Indian gaming provides a focused lens through which to examine dominant cultural attitudes and conflicting values as to what and who constitutes a Native American person in the United States in the 21st century.

On the surface, the controversy about Indian gaming involves economics and competition between groups for the profits of gaming operations. However, the controversy also involves much more than economic competition, since it touches upon taken-for-granted dominant ideas among non-Indian populations about how Native Americans should behave and appear. In the words of one commentator, "This is about greed—pure, unadulterated greed—and one more thing that's even more intolerable—racism" (Ribis and Traymar 1995:4). According to Kathryn Gabriel, in her study on Indian gaming:

> The opening of reservation casinos has been embroiled in controversy, locked up in courtrooms, and argued in Congress. The main conflict has been between individual states and the reservations within them. In part, it is a battle between sovereign entities, each determined to decide for itself what is to take place within its borders. It is also an economic struggle involving the redistribution of goods. Yesterday horses, blankets, rifles; today, hard cash. (Gabriel 1996:3)

On one side of the controversy about Indian gaming, among those who oppose it, some people think that if Native Americans make money they will become more active in politics, buy fancy cars, build big homes, travel, and send their children to off-reservation schools attended by non-Indian children. As a result, they will lose their traditional culture and so jeopardize what many people believe is their unique authenticity. The underlying assumption of these attitudes is that Indian peoples are only truly Indian if they are poor, out of sight and out of mind on faraway reservations, and not part of mainstream society. Others in our dominant society believe that Native Americans are not capable of running sophisticated business operations such as casinos, fearing that they will become victims of gangs and dishonest managers. The underlying assumptions here are that Native Americans are not smart enough, or certainly not as smart as other Americans, to run successful corporations, and that ruthless swindlers will constantly cheat them. And still others believe Native Americans should not make a profit from gambling because it can be labeled immoral and addictive behavior. The underlying assumption is that as a society we have a right to judge how others make their profits. As Kathryn Shanley notes in her article on Indian gaming, "When associated with the 'natural world,' Mother Earth, we are good Indians, but when we are involved in the business of making money from gambling, we are bad Indians" (Shanley 2000:93). In contrast to how many in mainstream society judge Indians involved in gaming enterprises, Las Vegas entrepreneurs and people such as Donald Trump, who is one of the largest individual casino operators in the world, are not stopped from running lucrative casinos on the grounds that gambling is morally wrong. Why should a different moral code be applied to Native Americans who are, after all, modeling their casino operations on highly successful capitalist undertakings?

On the other side of the Indian gaming controversy is the belief that Native Americans have been oppressed for too long and now deserve their newfound good fortune. Many of these people think that however tribal wealth is obtained, be it through gaming, mining, or processing of our toxic waste and garbage refuse, Native Americans should be free to make a profit and benefit from their commercial ventures. The underlying assumptions here are that the dominant population cannot dictate what constitutes "authentic" culture and correct values for Native Americans. Rather, indigenous peoples should be considered equal in every respect to non-Indians, and they should be able to take full advantage of the opportunities currently available to everyone else. That the manifestations of native cultural heritage, or at least what non-Indians think is native cultural heritage, may change as a consequence is really irrelevant. Thinking about this in another way, the laws in the United States now make it easier to obtain a divorce and for women to sue their husbands. These laws have unquestionably changed the way many ordinary Americans think about the family unit, and how we relate and interact with each other as family members. These changing legal relations between men and women are very different from what our parents or grandparents experienced. But most people would not say that our new set of social relations makes us no longer "authentic" citizens and that we should return to some historical notion of U.S. culture where everyone supposedly lived in idealized conventional family units with the father as the breadwinner and the wife as the economically dependent homemaker.

Those in support of Indian gaming also argue that past injustices perpetrated by whites against Native Americans may require making special rights available to Native Americans in order to level the playing field so they can achieve equality. One consequence of endorsing special treatment for indigenous peoples, even if it is only temporary, is that Native Americans are now receiving a greater visibility in mainstream society. This visibility, upheld on the legal grounds that Native American sovereignty exists and can now be used to legally justify certain segregated privileges denied ordinary American citizens, helps to create a new sense of injustice by many non-Indians who now claim they are being unfairly treated. In thinking about whether Native peoples should receive special benefits or not, the important point is to foreground the long history of discrimination, stigma, and prejudice that taints the non-Indian treatment of North American indigenous peoples, and which continues to make Native Americans the most impoverished and underprivileged minority group in the United States.

Whether one is for or against Indian gaming, what I hope to achieve with this book is to provoke thought about the various reasons for taking a particular side in the debate. There is no getting around the fact that at the beginning of the 21st century, gaming on Native American reservations is a booming industry. As a result, a few Native American tribes are now very rich and politically powerful. More specifically, some Native Americans can now participate in corporate America; they can buy land and invest in a range of economic ventures, build hospitals and schools for their people, and, for the first time since the precolonial era, be relatively self-sufficient and independent. If Indian gaming has brought a variety of economic, social, and cultural benefits to a few indigenous communities, why should anyone object to this gaming and all its apparent advantages?

Discussed in Chapter 1 are some of the misconceptions and stereotypes commonly raised by non-Indian populations who are against Indian gaming. Stereotypes are prejudicial labels applied to people, often with no foundation or justification. They are oversimplifications of reality, rooted in generalities, that gloss over the complexities of real life. Stereotypes are not insulated from cultural ideas, but are constructed by and animated through cultural values and beliefs. So while stereotypes are largely figments of a collective imagination, they are powerful and dangerous rhetorical tools when used to rationalize certain behaviors and attitudes. In World War II, for instance, Nazi Germany used stereotypes about the Jewish population to justify the extermination of millions of people. I am not suggesting that anyone today wants to kill off Native Americans. But I do want to stress that stereotypes and cultural assumptions among a dominant U.S. population about how Native Americans should or should not behave run very deep. As Native Americans begin to participate in corporate America and the question of who is an Indian becomes more difficult to answer, a sense is emerging that "they" are no longer recognizable as "authentic" Indians to "us." This blurring of ethnic identities is causing intense ruptures in the way many North Americans think about their colonial past and their postcolonial futures. These changing ideas challenge the basic notions of what it means to be a U.S. citizen and disrupt standard historical narratives of having descended from the Pilgrim Fathers and a European past and heritage.

As a consequence of casino operations, some of this country's poorest indigenous communities are now demanding a greater voice and presence in mainstream politics. "One tribe that spends lavishly for political clout in Washington is the Mississippi Band of Choctaw, operators of the $250 million-a-year Silver Star Casino. Asked about the $1 million he spends annually for Washington lobbyists, Choctaw Chief Philip Martin replied: 'I learned that from the white man. If you want support you are going to have to make friends'" (*Boston Globe,* March 13, 2001).

Native Americans' making "friends" in the halls of federal power is essential for their claim to independence from the federal government's paternalistic supervision over their lives and opportunities that has been in force for more than 200 years. What this independence means in terms of imagining the future of Native Americans, and U.S. society as a whole, in contemporary North America remains an open and highly contentious issue that affects us all.

The following pages are an exploration of some of the prevailing cultural assumptions, stereotypes, and myths about Native Americans that make Indian gaming so highly controversial and unsettling for many of "us." This book does not make an argument for or against Indian gaming, which I believe is ultimately up to the determination of each Indian nation. Rather, what I do in this book is explore why so many people in mainstream society feel that Indian gaming is a divisive and contentious issue that should be decided by a dominant majority non-Indian voice.

INDIAN GAMING IN CALIFORNIA

Each of the 50 states within the United States governs the form of gaming it allows within its jurisdiction. State governments argue that it is up to each specific state legislature to control what happens on Indian reservations within its territory. Some states are stricter than others, and in fact, only 29 states allow tribal governmental gaming (see Table I.1). So while historically the federal government has governed all matters pertaining to Native Americans through the Bureau of Indian Affairs, Indian gaming has forced state governments to become involved in recent years in their efforts to regulate gaming operations. For this reason, it must always be remembered that today's political and legal tensions over Indian gaming now exist between three major parties: tribal governments, state governments, and federal agencies.

In Chapter 4, I focus specifically on Indian gaming controversies in the state of California. Other state legislatures, such as those in Connecticut, Florida, and Minnesota, have sought to restrict Indian gaming operations since the early 1970s. However, nowhere has the Indian gaming discussion been so heated and involved so much public participation as it did in California in the late 1990s, when reservation gaming became one of the most debated and publicized issues of the decade. The state of California is the largest in the United States in terms of geographical size and population, with more than 34 million residents. California is home to 108 federally recognized tribes, with an additional 54 applying for federal recognition. In California, 50 tribes have casinos, and gaming revenues exceed $5 billion. In addition, tribal contributions to state political candidates have exceeded $42 million since 1999 (*Los Angeles Times*, November 5, 2002). So while almost half of the Native American population in the United States lives outside California in the states of Montana, Nevada, North Dakota, Oklahoma, and South Dakota, nonetheless California represents the state with potentially the highest profit margin for Native Americans, and in turn the biggest influence by Native Americans on county, state, and federal politics. Hence, California provides a significant and current illustration of one state grappling with the whole issue of Indian gaming and what it will and not allow in regulatory terms and cultural attitudes.

The National Indian Gaming Association in Washington, DC, and a few other agencies and organizations have conducted over the past decade a range of studies on the impact of Indian gaming. These studies tend to focus on the economic impact

TABLE I.1   TYPES OF INDIAN GAMING BY STATE

	No Federally Recognized Tribes	Federally Recognized Tribes, but no Gaming Allowed	Class II and III Gaming Allowed	Class II Gaming Only
Alabama				X
Alaska				X
Arizona			X	
Arkansas	X			
California			X	
Colorado			X	
Connecticut			X	
Delaware	X			
Florida				X
Georgia	X			
Hawaii	X			
Idaho			X	
Illinois	X			
Indiana	X			
Iowa			X	
Kansas			X	
Kentucky	X			
Louisiana			X	
Maine				X
Maryland	X			
Massachusetts		X		
Michigan			X	
Minnesota			X	
Mississippi			X	
Missouri		X		
Montana			X	
Nebraska				X
Nevada			X	
New Hampshire	X			
New Jersey	X			
New Mexico			X	
New York			X	
North Carolina			X	
North Dakota			X	
Ohio	X			
Oklahoma				X
Oregon			X	
Pennsylvania	X			
Rhode Island		X		
South Carolina				X
South Dakota			X	
Tennessee	X			
Texas				X
Utah		X		
Vermont	X			
Virginia	X			
Washington			X	
West Virginia	X			
Wisconsin			X	
Wyoming				X

of casinos on local businesses, labor markets, and the surrounding environment, as well as the extent to which casinos may change the level of tribal dependency on the federal government. While these studies are very important, as an anthropologist I am interested in how individuals experience these changes personally and as collective communities. I try to get the inside story, so to speak, on changing attitudes and values that surround these new commercial enterprises.

This case study uses the Chumash Indian casino in California as a way to look at the issue of Indian gaming in general, and more specifically at mainstream reactions to it. I focus upon the controversy surrounding the Chumash Band of Mission Indians in the County of Santa Barbara whose efforts to expand their casino have created a lot of local opposition. By looking at the way the controversy has been handled, and what local people such as politicians, competing business operators, and residents feel about having rich Indians in their own neighborhood, I build a more complex picture of dominant attitudes, how these attitudes may be currently changing, and what remains the same in terms of enduring myths about how Native Americans should and should not behave.

I have written this book in a style intended to be accessible to a general audience that is unfamiliar with the current topic and the necessary historical context. It is not intended to be either a comprehensive examination of Indian gaming or a detailed account of Native American affairs. Within the constraints of a case study, I've attempted to link current events to historical trends, local issues to national debates, and mainstream attitudes to government policy.

Bridging these different levels of analysis requires a combination of theories and methods from several disciplines. I have tried to bring abstract macro sociolegal theory to ground with a variety of ethnographic and qualitative methods. Personal interviews with casino operators, tribal members, and a variety of people living in the community around the Chumash reservation are used to highlight broader issues of citizenship, property rights, and self-determination. Policy discussions with Las Vegas entrepreneurs, politicians, and lawyers are combined with an analysis of mainstream media, newspapers, films, novels, and legal documents to show the interplay of cultural values and legal practices. My interpretations of archival materials are supplemented with statistical data from state and national surveys, as well as my own formal survey of local attitudes of over 700 Santa Barbara County residents in September 2002, which showed overwhelming opposition to the Chumash Casino expansion among those living within close proximity to the reservation (see Darian-Smith forthcoming). These surveys show the historical continuity of past and present attitudes toward Indian gaming. Together these disparate sources of information represent a wide breadth of official, institutional, and individual perspectives, opinions, and ideas about what constitutes Indian gaming and why it should or should not be allowed. By merging what are essentially cultural-anthropological practices with questions informed by sociolegal theory, I try to open a space where dominant assumptions about who should be in power and for whom the legal system works can be critiqued.

The heated disputes involving California's Proposition 5 in late 1998 and Proposition 1A in early 2000, each of which allowed Native Americans to operate Las Vegas–style gaming on their reservations, provide a site through which to examine how the power of global capital and global tourism, as epitomized by Las Vegas casino owners, is both competing with and supporting local struggles by native peoples to enter North America's corporate world. One of the reasons Indian gaming propositions in California have caused such huge public debates is that they challenge a dominant non-native public's beliefs about who can legitimately participate in entrepreneurial economic enterprises. Native American casino owners are confronting federal and state authorities in their attempts to establish casinos and compete for a casino clientele. In the process, Native American casino owners disrupt a prevailing social attitude that indigenous people should be dependent upon the government and should abide by its rules and regulations. "Rich Indians," the kind who own brownstone buildings in the nation's Capitol, challenge what many non-natives consider the "natural order of things" whereby certain people occupy high-paying jobs and certain people occupy low-paying jobs. The image of the rich Indian competes with the image of the Indian in popular culture who is typically poor, living on a reservation, not accessible, not participating in modern society, and certainly non-threatening in any concrete sense. The cultural work performed by popular images of Native Americans, which inadvertently reinforce ideas that indigenous peoples belong in positions of inferiority and submission, is subverted by the contrasting image of "rich Indians."

Casinos and tourism often go hand-in-hand. Many reservations with casinos have been attracting a great deal of interest from the general population because of their gaming operations, as well as a host of other attractions such as museums, cinemas, and outlet malls largely built and financed through gaming profits. On successful gaming and tourist reservations, there is a swelling sense of identity, pride, optimism in the future, and renewed nationalist spirit. In comparison, many of the tribes without gaming operations are becoming increasingly disillusioned by their marginalization from mainstream society and their inability to access the same resources as their more successful tribal neighbors. There is a growing disparity between rich and poor tribes, as well as in some cases between rich and poor members within a single tribe. This disparity is causing new cleavages and divisions within Native American populations, as well as between Native American populations and their surrounding non-native, less economically successful communities.

Historically, legal standards were set defining what a person must do to prove Native American descent. Under the Bureau of Indian Affairs, the standard was usually a one-fourth blood degree when determining the allocation of money for health care, housing, education, and so on. These legal standards have changed over time, but still involve "blood quantum" requirements and represent certain Western ideals of what constitutes an "authentic," and by implication "traditional," native person. However federally recognized Indian tribes retain, though the doctrine of sovereignty, the right to set their own criteria and standards for acknowledging membership, which often require proof of lineal descent and lesser emphasis on blood quantum levels. Needless to say, there has been conflict between the Bureau and some tribes over who should be classified as being Native American. In the past, these debates over authentic tribal ancestry were largely confined to mainstream legal arenas. But now tribes are disputing more often among themselves over these issues. The Catawba tribes of South Carolina, the Paiutes of Nevada, and the Tigua of Texas all debated the rules of blood quantum and tribal membership in 2001. According to reporter Hector Tobar, "Blood has become an obsession among nearly all of the nation's 550 officially recognized tribes" (*Los Angeles Times*, January 4, 2001). Because of the growing disparity between poor and wealthy native communities, the issue of membership has again become extremely heated at the beginning of the 21st century. "Money is the greatest attraction in the world," said Ralph Sturges, the longtime chief of the casino-owning Mohegan tribe in Connecticut. "Because Indians are making money, now it's a privilege to become one" (*The Day*, March 21, 2001).

Unfortunately, the growing disparities among native populations threaten to undermine advances currently being made toward building large-scale Native American social movements and advancing the acceptance and credibility of indige-nous people within mainstream society. An anthropological perspective asks: To what extent are the problems faced by Native Americans and the growing distance between rich and poor within their own communities mirroring the growing distance between rich and poor in our dominant society? Is this growing economic divide a feature of advanced capitalism that cannot be avoided? Or can we think of new solu-tions and new means to make sure there is some equity between all people so that everyone has access to basic rights such as health, education, job opportunities, and legal representation?

Questioning who is accepted as part of mainstream society also illustrates how we in wealthy Western nations continue to treat the indigenous people who first occu-pied the lands we now control. In the current phase of globalization, so often inter-preted as a breaking down of borders and barriers between people, there are also concurrently new divisions and barriers being built up between countries, communi-ties, and individuals. As Naomi Klein has argued:

> Globalization is now on trial because real people [are now] shut out of schools, hospitals, workplaces, their own farms, homes and communities. Mass privatization and deregula-tion have bred armies of locked-out people, whose services are no longer needed, whose basic needs go unmet. These fences of social exclusion can discard an entire industry, and they can also write off any entire country, as has happened to Argentina." (*Guardian Weekly*, October 17, 2002:23)

Some of the negative results of increasing globalization in the United States are increased policing of border controls and new forms of conservative and reactionary state nationalism. Remember, internal changes and pressures emerging from within any one country cannot, and should not, be separated from the pressures exerted by economic, political, and social forces outside a country. Unfortunately, this internal dimension of globalization is too often ignored. This book reflects upon how Native Americans' participation in corporate America represents a powerful internal chal-lenge to the dominant cultural understanding of what it means to be American and a citizen of the United States—an exploration that cannot be divorced from the larger context of challenges to state nationalism presented by a global political economy.

A NOTE ON LANGUAGE AND DEFINITIONS

Throughout the book I use a variety of terms that refer to the people who occupied lands prior to being colonized and controlled by Anglo-European administrations. In Africa, colonization began in the 16th century; in the United States and Canada, it occurred in the 17th century; and in Australia and India, it occurred in the late 18th century. Despite the different dates of occupation among colonial regimes, all com-monly referred to the indigenous people already living in colonized territories in derogatory terms such as *savages, barbarians,* and *Indians.* Such terminology is no longer acceptable. Instead a range of words is used to denote first peoples such as *indigenous, aborigine, First Nations,* and *Native American. First Nations* is the term most often used in reference to the indigenous peoples of Canada, and *aborigine* is most commonly used in referencing Australian Aborigines.

Indian is a highly loaded word, with connotations of prejudice and racism. Some Native Americans still refer to themselves as Indians, while others find the term highly offensive. In this book, I use the terms *Indian, Native American, indigenous,* and *First Nations* somewhat interchangeably. Still, it is important to note, as David Wilkins argues, that indigenous communities prefer to be referred to by their own names—Navajo, Dine, Ojibwa, Anishinabe, Sioux, or Lakota—since each group constitutes a unique political, social, and legal entity (Wilkins 2002).

Casino operations on tribal reservations are referred to as *Indian gaming.* I use this term because it is one used by tribal governments themselves. While it may not be considered politically correct, I believe it is respectful to use the terminology Native Americans themselves use until directed by them to do otherwise. Similarly, I remember when I first arrived in the United States in 1990, I was confused about whether to use the term *black* or *African American.* At a small post office I went to in south-side Chicago, I asked the owner what terminology she preferred. Her response was that she was *black* and that the term *African American* was generally not one she or her friends would use themselves. As she explained her view further to me, it became clear that for this woman, *black* was a powerful political statement that she used precisely because it references the enduring black-white racial politics of the contemporary United States. The term *Indian gaming* seems to carry a similarly charged political message, made potent precisely by its apparent political incorrectness.

Whatever terminology is used to talk about indigenous peoples, it is important to appreciate that all these words are generalized terms that do not account for the complexities of relations within and between people from different Native American tribes and nations. Just as there is no such thing as one singular U.S. culture, there is no such thing as one singular Native American culture. It is important for us not to think about Native Americans as a homogenous, united, and uniform group, even though the legal system treats native peoples this way and popular attitudes represent them this way.

In a similar vein, the insights presented in this book do not represent all non-native peoples. I am a white Australian woman who, before coming to the United States to train as a cultural anthropologist, practiced law. As a cultural anthropologist and lawyer, I attempt to read between the lines in examining some of the assumptions and attitudes that have become "common sense" in the public domain. My goal is to make readers think about what constitutes a Native American, what is at stake in the current politics of Indian gaming, and how law and popular opinion in the United States and elsewhere continue to shape the policies and opportunities for indigenous peoples as they seek to carve out sites of sovereignty, independence, and self-government.

1/Enduring Western Stereotypes of Native Americans

HISTORICAL MYTHS AND NAVIGATING THE FUTURE

In order to understand the debates surrounding Indian gaming, we need to get past the taken-for-granted ideas many Euro-Americans hold about Native Americans. We should approach the topic without preconceived ideas about how native peoples ought to act and behave. This chapter explores enduring ideas and conceptions about Native Americans in the dominant popular culture of the United States. I like to think of these ideas as *myths* about indigenous peoples, which does not mean that they are fairy tales or falsehoods. Rather, our whole understanding of the historical past is based on myths, be they about us or others. As Ronald Wright has argued:

> Myth is an arrangement of the past, whether real or imagined, in patterns that resonate with a culture's deepest values and aspirations. Myths create and reinforce archetypes so taken for granted, so seemingly axiomatic, that they go unchallenged. Myths are so fraught with meaning that we live and die by them. They are maps by which cultures navigate through time. (Wright 1992:5)

Myths reinforce stereotyped ideas and images about Native Americans. Many of these notions about native peoples have existed since the time of first contact and conquest by Europeans in the "New World" more than 500 years ago. Of course, these ideas have developed and changed over time to reflect the contemporary historical moment and socioeconomic frame. Attitudes existing in the 1700s could never be exactly the same as those held in the 1900s or today. That being said, there are certain myths and themes that have remained relatively constant in how the dominant Euro-American population viewed, and continues to view, the indigenous communities of this country. It is important to acknowledge and recognize these myths because in the current controversies surrounding Indian gaming, they resurface to fuel ignorance and misunderstanding.

AN INEVITABLE HISTORICAL TRAGEDY?

One of the most constant myths in the conventional history of the United States is that it was no one's fault that the Native American population dramatically declined over the past centuries. The facts of war, foreign diseases, and the deliberate killing of Indians by European colonists are overlooked in favor of the belief that native people are "naturally" inferior. This narrative accounts for their initial conquest by Europeans and helps to explain their assumed inability to live in the civilized and sophisticated world of the white man. This is the myth of "inevitable historical tragedy," sometimes known as "manifest destiny," which encourages us to expect that certain people, of particular ethnic background or racial characteristics, will live longer and more profitable lives compared to others who will not be able to keep up and will inevitably die out. This idea is often referred to as "social Darwinism" or "social evolutionism."

Responding to this myth, Jimmie Durham, a Native American activist, writes angrily:

> American Indians obviously cannot be called "Americans." We cannot, therefore, be considered politically. We must be spoken of mythically, as American Indians, or anthropologically, as "Amerinds." We are thereby effectively removed from the arena of political discourse in exactly the same way we are removed from artistic, literary, and cinematic discourse. Instead of fundamental human rights, we have more specialized and esoteric "Rights of Indigenous Populations." This is a set of rights, even now being formulated and articulated, which precludes intellectual consideration and substitutes sentimental feeling. European colonization of Africa and even the U.S. exploitation of Latin America are generally seen as being outrageous and intolerable. Our circumstance, on the other hand, is usually viewed as something of an "inevitable historical tragedy." (Durham 1992:430)

The myth of inevitable historical tragedy continues to permeate popular culture and dominant attitudes toward Native Americans today. There is a widespread and enduring belief that left to themselves, indigenous people will just die out and disappear. Rodman Wannamaker's book, *The Vanishing Race,* first printed in 1913 and rereleased in 1972, is one of many texts to affirm this idea; it incorrectly relies upon a social evolutionary model suggesting that indigenous people occupy a lower order of being and in a sense cannot keep up with modern, industrial society. *The Vanishing American,* a 1925 Hollywood movie, picked up this epic theme. Although the movie was sympathetic to the oppressed Indians, it nonetheless confirmed the idea that they have no place in contemporary society. A typical scene in the movie depicts a Navajo Indian boy silently watching a government agent as his horse is taken away, with the subtitle announcing, "Even in his short life, Nasja had learned that the white man must have his own way—that the Indian can only watch and endure, and dumbly wonder."

Hollywood movies from the 1990s reinforce the myth of inevitable historical tragedy, usually tying the fate of the native peoples with the environment and its degradation and abuse by industrial society, as discussed later. In short, the myth of Indians being profoundly different from whites and not part of modern society continues to saturate popular dominant attitudes toward this country's indigenous populations. Significantly for the purposes of this case study, it also shows up in the debates about Indian gaming and supports the mistaken belief that Native Americans do not belong in corporate America and would not survive in any case if they tried to become successful capitalists.

The narrative of inevitable historical tragedy is powerful and dangerous. It excuses both the federal government and wider U.S. society for its treatment of indigenous peoples in the past and, at the same time, places blame and responsibility on Native Americans for their current plight. The implicit message is: If "they" were equal to "us," so many of them wouldn't still be living in squalid poverty, on distant reservations, apparently unable or unwilling to participate in modern society. This misconception ignores the structural inequalities integral to our political, legal, and social system that make it easier for some people to take advantage of available opportunities than others. As the two economists, Terry Anderson and Dean Lueck, note:

> Traditional explanations for the lack of economic growth among Indians have typically focused on insufficient access to capital markets, low levels of education, poor endowments of natural resources, or Indians' goals and attitudes. To this list must be added the role institutions play in determining resource allocation. (Anderson and Lueck 1992:147)

In this context it is important to remember that attending college or university is a privilege, and the ability to attend says a lot about such things as one's socioeconomic class, family income, cultural beliefs, and the capacity to speak and write the English language. Attending college, and as a result increasing one's chances of obtaining a well-paying job, is not something that certain people naturally should do because they are somehow superior. Yet, Native Americans have more difficulty attending college than most and for reasons that have nothing to do with the quality or capacity of individuals. Rather, they have been subjected to long-standing discriminatory laws, forced to live on faraway reservations with little money for transportation, clothes, and books, and have had to take local, often poor-paying jobs close to home at an earlier age in order to supplement low family incomes—all of which are relevant factors to be considered.

INDIANS AS A FIGMENT
OF THE WHITE MAN'S IMAGINATION

Early Europeans at the time of discovery thought of the Americas as the *nuevo mundo*, or New World. In truth, it was a world as old as the one from which they sailed. The new world was called "America" after a Florentine merchant and slave trader, Amerigo Vespucci; it first appeared on a German map in 1507. The term *American Indians* gradually came into use to refer to the indigenous peoples of central and north America. The term *Indian* was first coined by Muslims to refer to the people of the "Sindh" river region, which is present-day India. Christopher Columbus, who was hired by King Ferdinand and Queen Isabella of Spain to discover a new route to China in 1492, mistakenly thought he had landed on the Indian subcontinent, when in fact he had landed at one of the present-day islands in the Bahamas. As a result of his navigational confusion, he described the indigenous people he encountered as *Indians*. This name has been used ever since to widely refer to all indigenous people throughout the Americas. Some people find this term pejorative and tainted with prejudice. As Leonare Keeshig-Tobias has commented, "How I loathe the term Indian. . . . 'Indian' is a term used to sell things—souvenirs, cigars, cigarettes, gasoline, cars. . . . 'Indian' is a figment of the white man's imagination" (cited in Wright 1992:ix).

Indeed, the idea of the "Indian" is very much a figment of the white man's imagination. First, there is no such thing as the Indian, just as there is no such thing as the European, the Asian, or the African. All these general terms mask the extraordinary complexity and diversity that exist among different peoples living across vast continents. From the perspective of most North Americans, there are few obvious differences between a German and a French person. Their countries lie side-by-side, and their peoples probably understand if not speak each other's language. However, German culture is very different from French culture; the two countries have different state religions, national foods, literature, music, traditions, holidays, and so on. To someone living in northern Europe, the differences between these two cultures and nationalities are enormous, and it is insulting to say the two are the same. Similarly, to equate an Inuit from northern Alaska with a person from the Seminole tribe in Florida can be perceived as extremely ignorant and offensive. My point is that although terms such as *Indian* and *Native American* are freely used as convenient shorthand, we all should be sensitive to the masking of complexity behind these crass generalizations.

At the time of first European contact with native peoples in North America, there were approximately 1,000 different tribes, representing a huge array of languages and numerous subdialects. Each of these tribes had its own religious practices, social structures, governmental organization, gender division, dress, customs, and rituals. Today, this number has declined to approximately 511 culturally distinct, federally recognized tribes and about an additional 200 unrecognized tribes. And of these remaining tribes, the populations of each have dramatically declined from the time of colonialization through disease and oppression over the past 300 years. But even with this vast decrease in numbers and the extermination of some tribes altogether, native people from one tribe are still unique as compared with people from another. Therefore, it is not appropriate to stereotype all Indians, either in the past or today, as living in teepees, wearing braids, and donning headdresses (see Figure 1.1). Teepees, braids, and headdresses are the usual symbols Euro-Americans associate with indigenous people, but they are actually linked to the Plains tribes that historically hunted buffalo and that differ greatly in dress, housing, and lifestyle from the tribes living on the east coast in Maine or Florida, near the Great Lakes, or in the Arctic region (Mihesuah 1996:20–21).

Second, it is important to be aware of the politics and power dynamics behind the use of the all-encompassing word *Indian*. As noted by Marchell Wesaw, former director of Education and Public Policy at Cultural Survival, an organization dedicated to "promoting the rights, voices, and visions of indigenous peoples since 1972":

> The "Indian" is a flexible notion capable of being whatever the White world wants or does not want. The Indian can be a Noble or Savage. Indians can be evil incarnate, scalping and torturing innocents, or they can be pure-hearted environmentalists saving the forests and weeping over urban pollution. "Indians" can be anything and everything White policies want them to be. At this level of imaging, the Indian becomes a stereotype. White society attempts to make "Indianness" part of mainstream culture, thereby validating the appropriation of Native land and resources. By making Native American cultures more of what White society wants, by making them "Indian" and assimilating the Indian into main-

Figure 1.1 Issue day at Pine Ridge Agency; Indians wait for their issue, 1890.

stream society, Whites begin to take care of the "Indian problem." The more the Indian is like the White and the White like the Indian, the less the White has to feel guilty for. By dealing in stereotype, White society does not have to confront the reality of broken treaties and stolen lands. (Wesaw 1995:8–9)

FIRST CONTACT AND IMPACT

North America was colonized by several European countries, each with their own particular agenda and reasons for exploration of and domination over the vast new world. The continent was first exploited and colonized by the Spanish who came up through central America and then Mexico in the 1540s, murdering Aztec and Inca peoples for their silver and gold along the way, making Spain the richest and most powerful European nation. At the same time that the Spanish conquistadors and missionaries were making their way north up the west coast through Texas and into what is now California, French explorers arrived in Canada. Like the Spanish, the French were motivated by a desire to own land and riches, to spread Catholicism, and to "civilize" the natives. In contrast to the Spanish and French, the Protestant Dutch colonies established on the eastern seaboard near New York were mainly interested in trading networks and focused primarily on the fur-trading business and the slave trade. The Dutch were not as interested in staking out property rights and establishing control over lands and indigenous peoples as they were in making a lot of money through quick venture arrangements.

The English came to the new world for yet different reasons. Many of the early English colonists were forced to flee England because of religious persecution; they had little choice but to come to the relatively unpopulated and "free" new world. The English who arrived at the two small eastern colonies at Jamestown and Plymouth in the late 16th and early 17th centuries successfully set up large settler colonies. Between 1607 and 1675, tens of thousands of English men and women migrated to North America to start new lives and seek their fortune by establishing basic agricultural farms and staking claims to freehold land.

English colonists gave little consideration to Native Americans in their colonizing practices. As a result of the new English colonies established in Virginia, Plymouth, Connecticut, Maryland, Rhode Island, and Massachusetts Bay, Native Americans succumbed to a range of newly introduced diseases such as smallpox, measles, typhoid, chicken pox, and scarlet fever. Most of those who survived disease were run off their land by colonists and pushed farther and farther westward. What happened in New England was typical of other colonized regions: "By the 1670s, the white population of New England had reached 55,000, and Puritan communities stretched for 50 miles along the Connecticut River valley. . . . [T]he Indian population in southern New England dropped from 120,000 in 1570, to 70,000 in 1620, to barely 12,000 in 1670" (Henretta et al. 1993:60). According to one commentator, "Native Americans, whose ancestors had lived on the American continents for millennia, found that they too were living in a new world, but for them it was a bleak, dangerous, and conflict-ridden place, rendered deadly by European diseases and the hardly less benign presence of thousands of armed settlers" (Henretta et al. 1993:60).

EARLY COLONISTS AND THEIR SHIFTING ATTITUDES TOWARD NATIVE AMERICANS

At first contact, natives were not always treated with hostility and aggression by Europeans, who at times considered them more of a curiosity than a threat. From the Renaissance period and the earliest encounters in the 15th and 16th centuries, there was certainly a strong sense that indigenous people were distinctly different from Europeans for a variety of reasons based on their appearance, dress, diet, social organization, and so on (see Sayre 1997; Jahoda 1999; Todorov 1999; Pagden 1993). However, these differences did not necessarily cause open prejudice and discrimination. The Dutch and Portuguese were more willing to mix socially with the Indians than the Spanish, and a significant number of recorded cases of intermarriage indicates some level of social acceptance. Even in Spain, whose conquistadors always maintained that indigenous people in the Americas were less than human, a serious religious debate raged in Valladolid between 1550 and 1551 over the nature of the new world "barbarians." The point I want to stress is that at first contact, not all colonial Europeans considered all natives with hostility and aggression. There were considerable differences in attitude among the colonial French, Dutch, Spanish, and English toward native peoples. These differences translated into different types of exchanges and social relations. (For a clear discussion of these different nationalist attitudes, see Peckham and Gibson 1969).

One of the Spanish clergy who differed from the conquistadors and advocated for a compassionate understanding of native people was Bartolemé de Las Casas. His mission was to diminish the differences between Europeans and Native Americans and argue for the civil and political rights of Indians. His claim was that the native population was essentially "men like us." Furthermore, he argued that over time they could be educated to uphold the Christian faith and cease to be considered strange or foreign (Pagden 1993:57). Certainly this attitude was still very colonial in that it was inherently based upon a sense of European superiority over native peoples. Nonetheless, Las Casas, in his now famous work *Historia de las Indias* (1527–1559), was one of the first to describe the sufferings of indigenous people at the hands of the Spanish, and the need to recognize them as legal equals with rights to land and resources. In a sermon in 1511, Las Casas asked:

> With what right and with what justice do you keep these poor Indians in such cruel and horrible servitude? By what authority have you made such detestable wars against these

people who lived peacefully and gently on their own lands? Are these not men? Do they not have rational souls? Are you not obliged to love them as yourselves? (cited in Pagden 1993:70–71)

Individuals like Las Casas who advocated sympathetic and compassionate attitudes toward natives held a similar position to some of the later 18th century Enlightenment intellectuals who argued that "savages" were in fact noble and to be admired for their apparently egalitarian societies devoid of class and religious divisions. The idealization of the "noble savage" attracted a significant following, particularly among French theologians and philosophers, as well as American revolutionaries such as Benjamin Franklin, who upheld Native American social organization as an icon of how America should govern itself (see Grinde and Johansen 1991; Johansen 1987). However, these sympathetic views were quickly drowned out by the very different opinions of the vast majority of Europeans living in north and central America. By the early 1700s, Spanish, Dutch, French, and English held similar attitudes toward the native peoples they encountered despite their various motivations for occupying the new world in the first place, and despite the diverse ways each nation set up its colonial outpost. By the second part of the 18th century, these attitudes had crystallized into a predominantly shared set of beliefs that indigenous peoples were wild people, apelike or childlike, little more than savages or beasts without religion, culture, or government. The German scholar Meiners stated in 1787:

> The Americans are unquestionably the most depraved among all the human, or human-like creatures of the whole earth, and they are not only much weaker than the Negroes, but also much more inflexible, harder, and lacking in feelings. Despite the fact that this communication contains only a few traits of the terrible portrait of the bodily and moral nature of Americans, one will nonetheless feel, and be astonished, that the inhabitants of a whole continent are so closely related to dumb animals. (cited in Jahoda 1999:21–22)

THE CIVILIZING PROCESS OF MASSACRES AND MISSIONS

The common belief among European settlers in the 18th and 19th centuries that natives were little more than animals was upheld in varying degrees. At one end of the spectrum, some Europeans believed that natives, despite being at a lower level of maturity, could be "civilized" through education and Christian evangelism. There was a vague notion that in time indigenous people might one day be able to participate in modern society as assimilated whites.

In 1819, the U.S. Congress established the "civilization fund" with the explicit purpose of promoting the education and "civilization" of Native Americans. This notion of civilizing took many forms, one of which was the conversion of indigenous people to Christianity. Throughout the 19th century, the church in conjunction with federal authority established many missions on Indian lands. Large numbers of Indians were converted, often under duress. Colonial powers also introduced boarding schools in the 1870s with the specific intention of removing young Indians from their families and homelands, and replacing their heritage and traditions with the values and lifestyle of "disciplinary" Christianity. Many young Native Americans, removed from their loved ones and often unable to communicate in English, suffered terrible emotional and physical hardships (see Figures 1.2 and 1.3). This systematic

Figure 1.2 The boarding school at Pine Ridge Agency, 1890–1891

removal of young people to distant boarding schools contributed to a breakdown of internal tribal relations and often destroyed the ritual succession of customs from one generation to the next. Moreover, many priests fathered children by young Indian women, who were often forced into sexual relations with them, creating a socially and culturally ambiguous generation of children. These disruptions to tribal life were extremely destructive in a variety of ways, the most obvious being the breakdown of established kinship networks. It has been estimated that by the end of the 19th century, there were at least 20,000 Indians registered in 148 boarding schools (Mihesuah 1996:41).

The idea that Indians required aid in order to be civilized was further confirmed in the treaty terms offered to many tribes in the westward expansion across the United States throughout the 19th century. By 1825, most U.S. Indian treaties included provisions for education and agricultural support in the form of teachers, missionary settlements, and sometimes basic equipment (see St. Germain 2001:101). However, these forms of aid were largely symbolic measures designed to assuage the guilt of an evangelical federal government bent at all costs on supporting westward expansion and the ultimate goal of populating the entire United States. More often than not this meant moving Indians off their lands to distant reservations on property that was practically useless, and which no one wanted at the time. The 1868 Report of the Indian Peace Commission stated:

> We do not contest the ever-ready argument that civilization must not be arrested in its progress by a handful of savages. . . . We earnestly desire the speedy settlement of all our territories. None are more anxious than we to see their agricultural and mineral wealth developed by an industrious, thrifty, and enlightened population. And we fully recognize the fact that the Indian must not stand in the way of this result. (cited in St. Germain 2001:102)

Treaties with Indians, both those initially entered into by the English in the early colonial period and the many made later by white Americans in the 19th century, officially recognized indigenous peoples as having legal rights. Treaties underscored that tribes were in fact sovereign nations, with an ability to sign away their existing privileges to land and resources. However, legal recognition of Indian sovereignty was very much ignored in practice. The U.S. government and its agents ultimately overlooked or overrode hundreds of treaties entered into in good faith by Native

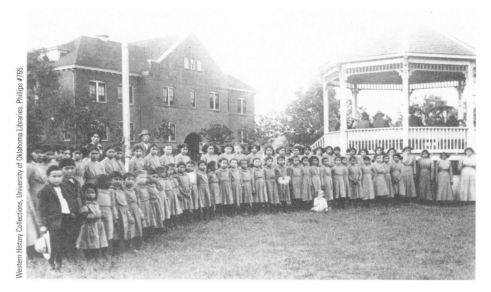

Figure 1.3 Students at Riverside Indian School at a band concert, Anadarko, Oklahoma, circa 1906

Americans. So although white Americans begrudgingly acknowledged the humanity of indigenous peoples by granting them limited legal rights, that acknowledgment was more a technical point that allowed the colonists to manipulate and exploit what were very dubious legal negotiations. While tribal governments have a very sophisticated system of checks and balances, and in effect their own legal systems, the white man's law was new and confusing to many native peoples. (See generally, on the impact of European law on Indian governance, Wunder 1996.) As legal historian Joseph Burke has argued:

> The nation long avoided facing Indian relations as a legal, political, or moral problem. The ambivalent Indian policy of the federal government, the irresistible push of white settlers, and the official "willingness" of the tribes to sell their lands long hid the conflict between the theory and practice of our Indian relations. In theory, the government treated the tribes as sovereign nations, purchasing only the lands they chose to sell and guaranteeing forever their title to the lands they chose to keep. In practice, the constant encroachment of white settlers, which the state governments would not and the federal government could not prevent, made a mockery of Indian sovereignty by forcing tribes to sell lands they wanted but could not peacefully keep. Written treaties that spoke of Indian nations, Indian boundaries, and Indian political rights remained on file, while time and the lack of records concealed the bribery, threats, and force that so often preceded their signing. Because the Indians, under pressure, usually sold the lands that the settlers demanded, the President, the Congress, and the Supreme Court could maintain the formal position that cession had been voluntary. (Burke 1996:137)

In chapter 2, I discuss at some length the abuse of western law and the paternalistic relationship by which the federal government came to oversee and manage Native Americans through the Bureau of Indian Affairs.

In stark contrast to the paternalistic attitudes toward indigenous peoples that justified a need to "civilize" them, some colonists believed the natives were ignoble, beyond redemption, and could never be improved. These colonists argued that the natives should be allowed to die out or become extinct, since they were considered little more than beasts or animals at a lower level of being. From the 16th century on, some Europeans even thought Indians were man-eating cannibals who enjoyed the flesh of their enemies in revengeful, ritualistic ceremonies. Gruesome tales of blood and guts circulated throughout Europe and provided a titillating backdrop to the common European understanding of the new world. While no concrete evidence existed to support the claim of cannibalism, nonetheless some European colonists used the myth to help justify their actions of deliberate killing or the passive ignoring of disease, poverty, and starvation that afflicted many Native Americans. (On cannibalism, see Jahoda 1999:97–112; Pagden 1993; Célestin 1996; Lestringant 1997; Barta 1997).

By the 19th century, the idea of American natives being equivalent to fierce animals or even cannibals had greatly diminished, though some novelists, such as James Fenimore Cooper with his famous book *The Last of the Mohicans* (1826), and some anthropologists, such as Alfred Métraux, kept it alive well into the early 20th century. One reason for this shifting attitude toward Native Americans was that the dominant white population no longer considered them a threat to the expansion of American settlement. Decimated by disease and war, removed from their land and placed on reservations, many Native Americans were in no condition to fight the powerful force of white settlement and capitalism as epitomized by the railroads that crisscrossed the nation by the end of the 19th century. More often than not, by the mid-1800s, Indians were thought of by white Americans as essentially pathetic and obsolete reminders of some sort of prehistoric age. They were no longer a military threat. The big question was what to do with them administratively, and how best to keep them contained on faraway reservations. Contact between Indians and non-Indians was severely reduced. The number of Indians had declined in comparison to the burgeoning white population, and the presence of Indians in urban contexts was a rarity. The little interaction that did occur between white and indigenous peoples took place in predominantly rural environments such as supply stations, on ranches, and amongst pioneering settlements in the expanding frontier regions of the west (Figure 1.4).

FRONTIER EXPANSION AND WILD WEST SHOWS

Popular attitudes among the Anglo-American population toward Native Americans supported the myth of inevitable historical tragedy. The frontier expansion of whites across the vast plains of the Midwest brought death and disease to many tribes and helped substantiate a 19th-century romanticized ideology that involved the foreseeable Indian extinction. Conquering nature, and by implication the native peoples who inhabited the wild frontier, was a central theme and mission for the new white American nation and its escalating nationalist spirit (see Frederick 1983; Dorst 1999; Wilton and Barringer 2002; Sandweiss 2002). The paintings of George Catlin in the first half of the 19th century and the photographs of Edward S. Curtis in the later 1880s and 1890s helped reinforce the notion of Indian nobility before the corruption and contamination of white civilization. Curtis played tricks with his photographs

Western History Collections, University of Oklahoma. Cunningham-Prettyman #103.

Figure 1.4 Cowboys at dinner on the Turkey-Creek Ranch, Oklahoma, circa 1885

and was known to touch up his negatives and erase any modern objects that would detract from images of Native Americans as he imagined them to be before contact with whites. In his 1914 ethnographic film "In the Land of the Headhunters," he showed northern Native Americans whale hunting when in fact the whale used was leased and already dead, and the traditional clothes they wore were made for the film and were no longer worn in real life.

Ironically, Curtis's romanticized soft-focus sepia prints, which deliberately set out to record the last of the "vanishing" Indians, were sponsored by J.P. Morgan, financial baron and financier for the great railroad industry (Figure 1.5). More than any other feature of the changing western landscape, railroads heralded the removal of Native Americans from their lands to designated reservations and the deliberate policies of the federal government for the dismantling of native cultures. Catlin's views were shared by many:

> Nature has nowhere presented more beautiful and lovely scenes, those of the vast prairies of the West, and of *man* and *beast* no nobler specimens than those who inhabit them—the *Indian* and the *buffalo*—joint and original tenants of the soil, and fugitives together from the approach of civilized man; they have fled the great plains of the West, and under an equal doom, they have taken up their last abode, where their race will expire and their bones will bleach together. (cited in Moses 1996:14)

The mythic West played a pivotal role in the popular imagination of those living in the urban and industrialized east. The historian Frederick Jackson Turner captured the moment in his hypothesis of "frontier America" in the 1880s. Jackson argued that American was a virgin continent where civilization (Europeans) met and ultimately conquered savagery (Indians). The collision between Europeans and Indians happened on the frontier, which was a fictitious geographical site that slowly moved from east to west as pioneers began to settle, farm, and tame the wild lands. According to Turner, this encounter with savagery helped forge the unique character

Alfred A. Hart Photograph Collection, Stanford University Archives.

Figure 1.5 Union Pacific Railroad work crews

and traditions of Americans. "Frontier America" became a central motif in under-standing the rugged individualism, defense of personal freedoms, sense of egalitari-anism, and suspicion of government that many commentators since Turner have pointed to as indicators of the exceptional American spirit.

Helping this sense of unique purpose and ideological fervor were men such as William Frederick Cody, better known as Buffalo Bill, who was born west of the Mississippi River in Iowa in 1846. Apart from serving in the Civil War, Cody had many jobs, including mounted messenger, Pony Express rider, gold prospector, and trapper. He also operated a hotel and hunted buffalo for the railroad, which, because of his reputed success, earned him the name Buffalo Bill. He became a legendary fig-ure of the "Wild West," merging fiction with reality. By 1870, Buffalo Bill had become such a celebrity that Ned Buntline featured him in an extensive series of cheap novels about his wild adventures and life on the frontier (see Figures 1.6 and 1.7). These legends merged with actuality when, three weeks after the total destruc-tion of Custer and his troops at Little Bighorn in 1876, Cody killed the Sioux chief Yellow Hand in a hand-to-hand fight.[1] Taking the "first scalp for Custer" while

[1]Under treaty in 1868, the federal government granted the Sioux Indians land called the Black Hills. For the Sioux, these hills were considered a special spiritual site. However, by 1872 rumors began that the hills contained gold, which was endorsed by General Custer in 1874. The federal government offered to buy back the land, but the Sioux refused. This caused the government to issue a warning, stating that all Sioux not living on reservations were to be considered "hostile." Numerous battles then occurred, the most famous being the battle of Little Bighorn in 1876. In this battle, under the leadership of Sitting Bull, the Sioux dealt General Custer and the U.S. army its greatest defeat. However, the retaliation was immense, and the U.S. army eventually forced the Sioux onto reservations.

Figure 1.6 Cover of Buffalo Bill novel, California Joe's War Trail

dressed in his stage *vaquero* outfit, Cody publicized his feat to legendary proportions, much to the delight of an ever-adoring audience.

In 1883 Cody took his legendary status to new levels. In order to exploit his growing fame and entrepreneurial interests, he staged his first Wild West Show, which further elevated his stature throughout the United States and Europe. These shows, which were a mixture of rodeo and circus, were full-blown extravaganzas featuring horsemen, sharpshooters, and more importantly, Indians. According to a reporter of the times, the show began with "a pony bare-back riding race between Indians and went on to a climax with a grand realistic battle scene depicting the capture, torture and death of a scout by savages; the revenge, recapture of the dead body and a victory of the government scouts." The performance ended with a "startling, soul-searching attack" by Indians on a stagecoach that was repulsed by Buffalo Bill and his cowboy friends (cited in Moses 1996:1).

One of the key features of the Wild West Shows was the participation of "real" Indians, which gave the battle scenes an air of authenticity and legitimate "wildness." Although Indians had been employed in ethnological exhibitions, circuses, carnivals, medicine shows, and plays since the 1840s, it was not until Cody's Wild West Shows that they began to feature as prominent individuals in their own right and grant the shows additional fame and notoriety. These Indians were called Show Indians. The most famous participant in Buffalo Bill's entourage was Chief Sitting Bull, who

Western History Collections, University of Oklahoma Libraries. Buffalo Bill #58.

Figure 1.7 Cover of
Buffalo Bill novel,
Silverblade, the Hostile

toured under duress with the company in the summer of 1885. Sitting Bull was associated in the minds of Americans with the death of General Custer at Little Bighorn.
In the show, he was dressed in his full tribal regalia of buckskin, paint, and feathers;
when he trotted out to face the booing crowds, he was considered an object of men-
acing and dangerous exotica.

The crowds loved to see Sitting Bull and paid handsomely to have their photographs taken with him (see Figure 1.8). At a time of no television and moving pic-
tures, these photographs served as mementos of the performance and, more
metaphorically, as symbols of the so-called reconciliation between natives and civilization. Removed from their homelands and dressed as objects of curiosity, Show
Indians were depersonalized, dehumanized, and decontextualized from their own
cultural heritage. Photos brought the dangerous Indian into the domestic arenas of
private homes and family albums. Such stylized photos were one more emblematic
act whereby Native Americans were ideologically tamed and disciplined by white
populations.

Cody's Wild West Shows started to make him considerable fame and fortune. By
1885 his shows had played to over a million people. He decided to take his entourage
of cowboys and Indians to England to Queen Victoria's Jubilee celebrations in 1887,

Western History Collections, University of Oklahoma Libraries. Finney #23.

SITTING BULL   BUFFALO BILL

Figure 1.8 Studio portrait of Sitting Bull and Buffalo Bill

and was there received with considerable excitement and acclaim. The Queen recorded her experiences after seeing one of Cody's shows:

> We sat in a box in a large semi-circle. It is an amphitheatre with a large open space, all the seats being under cover. All the different people, wild, painted Red Indians from America, on their wild bare backed horses, of different tribes—cow boys, Mexicans, etc, all came tearing round at full speed, shrieking and screaming, which had the weirdest effect. An attack on a coach and on a ranch, with an immense deal of firing, was most exciting, so was the buffalo hunt, and the bucking ponies, that were almost impossible to sit. The cow boys are a fine looking people, but the painted Indians, with their feathers, and wild dress (very little of it) were rather alarming looking, and they have cruel faces. . . . Their War Dance, to a wild drum and pipe, was quite fearful, with all their contortions and shrieks, and they came so close. "Red Shirt," the Chief of the Sioux tribe, was presented to me and so were the squaws, their papooses (children), who shook hands with me. (cited in Moses 1996:54–55).

Red Shirt, a Sioux chief, toured with Cody in the United States as well as in England. In London he made a huge impression, talking with politicians such as William Gladstone, and socializing with royalty such as the Prince of Wales and his family. Red Shirt was often cited in the British papers for his commentary on the

United States and his opinions on the future of Native Americans, and by 1893, when he appeared at the Colombian Exposition, he had become the most famous Show Indian in the world. Red Shirt enjoyed meeting the Queen and played up to the pomp and circumstance and the media interest. Interestingly, Black Elk, another of Cody's Show Indians, was not so impressed with being a stage performer. He recorded the Queen saying the following in a speech addressed to the Indians:

> I have heard about some people that were in America and I heard that they were called American Indians. Now I have seen them today. America is a good country and I have seen all kinds of people, but today I have seen the best looking people—the Indians. I am very glad to see them. *If I owned you Indians,* you good looking people, I would never take you around in a show like this . . . as beasts to show to the people. (cited in Moses 1996:53; my italics)

For the hundreds of Indians employed by Cody and other show entrepreneurs between 1883 and 1933, performing offered them an option away from the grim conditions of their remote and distant reservations. Wild West Shows granted a few Native Americans the opportunity to travel and earn meager wages. However, there were also explicit instances of exploitation and abuse. Many Indians did not receive full compensation for their work. More importantly, while a few Show Indians, such as Sitting Bull and Red Shirt, made a name for themselves as solo performers, their fame came at a cost. The general assumption was that, as Queen Victoria noted in her speech to the performers, Indians were "owned" by the U.S. government. Indian performers, consciously or not, reinforced stereotypes about native peoples as inferior beings and as chattels of show managers such as Cody. Whether depicted as savage, fierce, or childlike, Indians were above all presented as objects of curiosity belonging to a very different age and society. Seeing them dressed in war paint and feathers, people found it difficult to imagine them functioning in modern urban cities, traveling unattended, and managing their own performances. What concerns us for the purpose of understanding the current debates surrounding Indian gaming is that remnants of the 19th-century stereotype that Native Americans are incapable of functioning in modern society prevails to this day. This stereotype has mostly been sustained through Hollywood films, and what some Native Americans term "Indian biz," which refers to the enormous commercial industry that packages and markets items supposedly related to indigenous cultures.

HOLLYWOOD AND CONTEMPORARY STEREOTYPES OF INDIGENOUS PEOPLES

Native Americans continue to be objects of curiosity to non-Indian populations. Certainly specific stereotypes and ideas about what and who Native Americans are have changed over time to reflect contemporary perspectives and attitudes. Many images and perceptions about Native Americans today reflect a more positive outlook than in the past and attempt to praise and compliment indigenous cultures. One of the biggest changes, according to one social historian, is that:

> In the course of the 20th century the old image of the cruel and worthless savage had gradually become inverted and romanticized into that of the "Native American." They are now

seen as having been brace, clean-living peoples whose practices were a model of environmental preservation. (Jahoda 1999:24)

This newfound, but largely romanticized, respect for native peoples' connection with the land and environment emerged in the 1970s in conjunction with the civil rights movement and an increasing awareness of ethnic diversity and alternative lifestyles. In 1971, the Keep America Beautiful advertising campaign produced a famous television commercial targeting pollution and calling for a stop to the abuse of the environment. The commercial employed the actor Iron Eyes Cody, who interestingly followed the profession of his Cherokee Indian father who performed in circuses and Wild West Shows. In the TV commercial, Iron Eyes Cody, who quickly became know as the "Crying Indian," is shown standing beside a road, silently viewing a litter-strewn landscape. A single tear rolls down his check as passengers in a speeding car toss more garbage out the window and it lands at his feet. As Iron Eyes stares directly at the viewer, the voice-over says, "Some people have a deep, abiding respect for the natural beauty that was once this country, and some people don't." As anthropologist Shephard Krech has noted, "Through the Crying Indian, Keep America Beautiful cleverly manipulated ideas deeply ingrained in the national consciousness. The central idea is that on matters involving the environment, [the Indian] is pure . . ." (Krech 1999). This nostalgic belief in the ecological and spiritual purity of Native Americans saturates mainstream media. A 2002 article in the *Los Angeles Times,* written by a mother disturbed by pollution in the playground, makes the following statement (notice the use of language that acknowledges that Native Americans really own the country, but at the same time suggests that Native Americans are now dead and gone):

> I remember the Indian on the TV of my childhood. He cried at the thought of people littering *his* beautiful America. . . . It was his world that I fell in love with, his vision that I want to be safe for my son and my unborn child. . . . *I miss the Indian. I wish he were with us today,* teaching a new generation to take care of our land. (*Los Angeles Times,* September 7, 2002; my italics)

The idea of Native American spiritual purity and indigenous peoples' unique relationship with the land permeates the "new age" movement that became popular in the United States in the 1970s and 1980s. Richard Kyle argues that the movement recognized a relationship between nature and spirituality. "For the first time, many Americans were introduced to crystals and channeling. Reincarnation staged a comeback. Shaminism and Native American spirituality captured the imagination of many. People turned from traditional medicine and embraced holistic health practices" (Kyle 1995:1). It is, of course, very difficult to describe and analyze the complex and diverse movement known as the "new age." Many books and articles have been written on the subject. The alternative perspectives to which people connected with the movement subscribe span the fields of medicine, religion, environmentalism, self-help, and community building. It is important to note that indigenous spirituality has played a very important role in the general movement in the United States, as well as in the movement in Europe, Canada, and Australia. Following are two comments by "new agers" that epitomize the general sentiment about Native Americans being role models in a perceived need to return to nature and a more organic sense of community. Notice in these two statements the appropriation of Native American knowledge and Native American people as a single group, and how these speakers feel in some way authorized to speak on behalf of all indigenous peoples in the United States:

> It's like coming back to earth, coming back to what Native Americans were all about—living in oneness and harmony with the universe, not in disconnection with it. . . . [I]t's a celebration of . . . the earth, to give the earth thanks for all the things it gives us . . . that we don't really think about. . . . To give back and give thanks to the earth, and be more of that one community, for that one, that oneness. That community that people are looking for. (interviewee cited in Bloch 1998:65–66)

> Rainbow gatherings are like . . . the Indians [sic]. . . . [T]he Indians prophesied that there would be a tribe of people when the earth was weeping and the things were getting really bad on the earth, here would be a tribe of people to come . . . [A] great Indian leader saw this in a vision, and they would be called the Rainbow People, and these people would realize that we have come back to the earth. (interviewee cited in Bloch 1998:111–112)

The increasing interest by white Americans over the past two decades in Native American peoples and their cultures has translated into an enormous commercial industry that seeks to "capture the spirit" of indigenous cultures. Business is booming with respect to products connected with Indians who supposedly represent the opposite of urban white populations obsessed with making money and with material possessions. Nowhere is this more obvious than in the health and beauty industry. The irony is that today:

> consumers can eat, drink and dress "Indian" . . . one can wear Cherokee clothing, Seneca socks and Apache boots. During the day this consumer can drink native teas and snack on Hopi Blue Popcorn. . . . [T]o be "naturally" clean, one can shampoo with Native American Naturals and bathe with Zuni soaps. For one's head cold he or she can take medicines from Turtle Island. One can drive a Chief Grand Cherokee or Pontiac [jeep] to and from work. And one's home can be decorated in Southwestern accents and Mohawk carpets. In short, the consumer does not have to be born into a Native American clan or "tribe"; he or she can just buy one. This "purchase" is not all that far from the assimilation policies of the "frontier" days. (Wesaw 1995:9)

However, as many social critics note, "While these new images have been extensively exploited commercially, there is little indication that they have led to a greater understanding of, or respect for, Indian cultures" (Jahoda 1999:24). According to Wesaw, "The commercial use of Native American spiritual beliefs [has a] major impact on Native American cultures: these practices deny the very existence of traditional Native American beliefs as valid ways of life today. They do not foster acceptance of Native American lifestyles—they trivialize them" (Wesaw 1995:9–10). More importantly, these images of natural indigenous products and unique spirituality still posit Native Americans as opposite to white Americans. In other words, "Indian biz" flourishes precisely because all things associated with Native Americans continue to be considered fundamentally different, removed from urban city life and the functioning of modern capitalism, and representative of life in a comparatively simple and implicitly inferior world. This construction of the "Other" as a contrast to ourselves is what the theorist Edward Said has called "Orientalism" (Said 1978). For many non-Indian peoples, who are increasingly disillusioned with capitalist ethics, materialism, lack of family networks and support, and the general degradation of the environment, Native Americans represent both a romanticized golden past and a hope for a return to a simpler life in the future. White Americans need the myth of the "Indian" as being, in a profound sense, premodern and spiritual precisely because this myth performs vital cultural work.

At the same time, by making Native American spirituality and cultural uniqueness more accessible to mainstream society, the very differences that white society finds so fascinating and alluring are reduced to commercial commodities, to be purchased, appropriated, and controlled through the processes of consumption. As Ward Churchhill, a Keetoowah Band Cherokee and one of the most outspoken of all Native American activists, writes in his powerful book *Fantasies of the Master Race,* these current forms of appropriation of "Indianness" are "genocide of an extremely sophisticated type, to be sure, but . . . genocide nonetheless" (Churchill 1992).

Poet Wendy Rose epitomizes the problems for Native Americans seeking equality with non-Indians in professional occupations. As she notes, audiences react differently to her for no reason other than the fact that she is Native American:

> As a poet, I am continually frustrated by the restrictions placed on my work by the same people who insist that poets should not be restricted. It is expected—indeed *demanded*—that I do a little "Indian-dance," a shuffle and scrape to please the tourists (as well as the anthropologists). Organizers of readings continually ask me to wear beadwork and turquoise, to dress in buckskin (my people don't wear much buckskin; we've cultivated cotton for thousands of years), and to read poems conveying pastoral or "natural" images. I am often asked to "tell a story" and "place things in a spiritual framework." Simply *being* Indian—a real, live, breathing, up-to-date Indian person—is not enough. In fact, other than my genetics, this is the precise opposite of what is desired. The expectation is that I adopt, and thereby validate, the "persona" of some mythic "Indian being" who never was. The requirement is that I act to negate the reality of my—and my people's—existence in favor of a script developed within the fantasies of our oppressors. (Rose 1992:413)

In recent years, Hollywood has contributed to these shifting ideals from Indian savagery to Native American spirituality and environmental purity (see Kilpatrick 1999; Rollins and O'Connor 1998). In contrast to the Hollywood westerns of the 1950s and 1960s, where Indians were relegated to the roles of marauding enemies or faithful and subservient followers, contemporary films such as *Dances with Wolves* (1990), *The Last of the Mohicans* (1992), *Pocahontas* (1995), and *The Indian in the Cupboard* (1995) seek to show the positive value in Native American cultures. In the current political climate where white Americans constantly uphold the need to respect difference and cultural diversity, these films demonstrate in various ways the usefulness of "going Indian." Each emphasizes the need to listen to our Indian "friends" and learn from their inherent knowledge about mother nature and the environment—knowledge sorely lacking in modern industrialized society. In a sense, Native Americans are seen as white society's saviors, the last remaining key to redemption and a future free of anxiety, pollution, and complexity. While the directors' intentions in these films from the 1990s can be construed as well-meaning and sympathetic, the end result is simplistic tales full of objectified and commercialized caricatures of Native Americans. By depicting Indians as "free spirits," even though ultimately subjugated to control by whites (i.e., locked up, as in the film *The Indian in the Cupboard*), the contradictory and uneasy image of natives as both noble and savage again surfaces to reinforce the inability of the dominant popular culture to imagine native peoples as equal and fully functional citizens of the United States. In the words of Michael Riley, anthropologist and museum curator:

> Native America is an ongoing reinvention, perhaps one of mass media's most enduring and fanciful creations. In the end, the many faces of Native America, as mediated identities, must be understood in terms of the times and circumstances, as well as the motivations, of those who are representing the past. Thus in the cinema the objectification of Native Americans becomes a path toward a form of "ownership" by the dominant culture. . . . [O]ne of the crucial characteristics is the persistence with which Native America has come to symbolize simultaneously both nobility and savagery, alterity and common humanity. (Riley 1998:70)

INDIAN GAMING AND ITS UNSETTLING IMPACT TODAY

Indian gaming presents an unsettling set of images about Native Americans that does not fit easily with perceptions held by the dominant popular culture. Neither the images of natives as savage, oppressed, and pathetic on the one hand, nor as pure, natural, and spiritual on the other, fit in the context of Indian gaming. The cultural myth of inevitable historical tragedy or manifest destiny, whereby Indians are believed to be destined to fall behind whites and ultimately doomed to die out or vanish, is proving to be just that—a myth constructed by the dominant society in an effort to control and justify the enduring inequalities and injustices that permeate our legal system and social landscape. Moreover, the cultural myth of Indians as spiritual, pure, and connected to nature, land, and family is no longer sustainable in the face of Native Americans participating in contemporary society and behaving as savvy business people. Running lucrative casinos, bringing legal actions against government agencies and business competitors, negotiating with politicians, and influencing the future direction of mainstream political party policies are not typical ways in which our dominant society imagines Native Americans acting. In short, Indian gaming, and the newfound economic, political, and cultural independence that it brings to some individuals and tribes, destabilizes and undermines the carefully constructed images about Native Americans that we have become used to through contemporary film and mainstream media avenues.

Recognizing and understanding the power of our cultural myths about Native Americans is the first necessary step in approaching the topic of Indian gaming from a critical and thoughtful perspective.

SUGGESTED FURTHER READING

Churchill, Ward (1992) *Fantasies of the Master Race: Literature, Cinema and Colonization of American Indians.* Monroe, Maine: Common Courage Press.

Grinde, Donald A. and Bruce E. Johansen (1991) *Exemplar of Liberty: Native America and the Evolution of Democracy.* Los Angeles: American Indian Studies Center, UCLA.

Jahoda, Gustav (1999) *Images of Savages: Ancient Roots of Modern Prejudice in Western Culture.* London and New York: Routledge.

Kilpatrick, Jacquelyn (1999) *Celluloid Indians: Native Americans and Film.* Lincoln and London: University of Nebraska Press.

Krech, Shepard (1999) *The Ecological Indian: Myth and History.* New York: W.W. Norton.

Lestringant, Frank (1997) *Cannibals: The Discovery and Representations of the Cannibal from Columbus to Jules Verne.* Translated by Rosemary Morris. Berkeley: University of California Press.

Mihesuah, Devon A. (1996) *American Indians: Stereotypes and Realities.* Atlanta: Clarity Press.

Moses, L. G. (1996) *Wild West Shows and the Images of American Indians 1883–1933.* Albuquerque: University of New Mexico Press.

Pagden, Anthony (1993) *European Encounters with the New World.* New Haven and London: Yale University Press.

Peckham, Howard and Charles Gibson (1969) *Attitudes of Colonial Powers toward the American Indian.* Salt Lake City: University of Utah Press.

Rollins, Peter C. and John E. O'Connor (eds) (1998) *Hollywood's Indians: The Portrayal of the Native American in Film.* Lexington: The University Press of Kentucky.

Todorov, Tzvetan (1999) *The Conquest of America: The Question of the Other.* University of Oklahoma Press.

Wright, Ronald (1992) *Stolen Continents: The Americas through Indian Eyes since 1492.* New York: Houghton Mifflin.

2/Law and the Management of Indigenous Peoples

INTRODUCTION

In the last chapter we saw how Native Americans, since first contact with Europeans in the 15th century, have been treated with an ironic mixture of contempt, pity, as well as admiration by colonial powers. Non-Indian Americans have either admired indigenous peoples for their relationship to the environment, their spiritual connections to the land, and their sense of community justice and equality (see Grinde and Johansen 1991), or vilified them with charges of lack of education, heathen behavior, and essential inferiority. These two polarities of opinion have oscillated over time, reflecting the contemporary values and shifting social norms of any given historical period. Whatever the current vogue of thought, Euro-Americans have in some profound way always considered Native Americans different from the white population, and taken an active role in marginalizing them from mainstream society. Whether positive or negative conceptions of Native Americans prevail at any point in time, both reinforce the sense that Native Americans are not considered "ordinary" citizens of this country, and accordingly are not able to participate in the legal processes of democracy that most Americans take for granted. This sense of Native Americans' exclusion from mainstream society endures in the 21st century, with many non-Indians confused over whether Native Americans pay taxes, can vote, are bound by the laws of the United States, or should be treated as equals when it comes to such things as employment opportunities or health policies (see Figures 2.1 and 2.2).

In this chapter we turn to the United States' legal system to understand how it reflects and also helps shape prevailing attitudes by the white population toward Native Americans. The history of Indian law is extremely complicated, and a large number of books have been written on the topic (see in particular Wilkinson 1987; Washburn 1995; Wilkins 1997; Deloria and Wilkins 1999; Deloria and Lytle 1998; Carrillo 1998; Pommersheim 1995). The details of this legal history are well beyond the scope of my case study, but in any discussion of law, no matter how brief, it is clear that law was, and remains, an essential tool by which our dominant society institutionalizes and rationalizes ongoing injustices and discriminations against minority peoples. These minority groups have historically been women, the elderly,

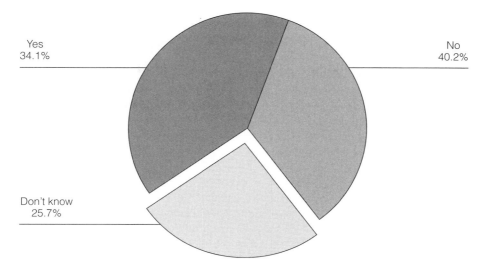

Figure 2.1 Do Native Americans pay taxes? This chart represents results from a phone survey I conducted of more than 700 respondents in Santa Barbara County, September 2002. It shows that nearly 66 percent of those interviewed incorrectly believe Native Americans do not pay taxes or are unsure whether they pay taxes. (See Darian-Smith forthcoming.)

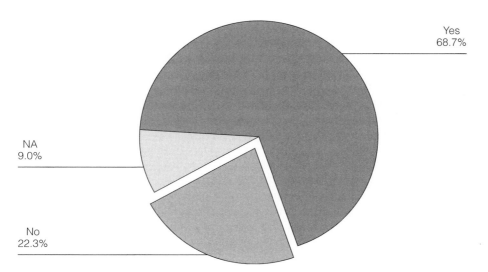

Figure 2.2 Are Native Americans governed by law? This chart represents results from a phone survey I conducted of more than 700 respondents in Santa Barbara County, September 2002. It shows that more than 30 percent of those interviewed incorrectly believe Native Americans are not governed by law or are not sure whether they are governed by law. (See Darian-Smith forthcoming.)

the mentally handicapped, as well as people identified for their religious or ethnic affiliations such as Jews, Chinese, Muslims, African Americans, and Native Americans. If we are to be thinking, savvy members of our society, we must recognize that law is not free from relations of power. With respect to the current laws surrounding Indian gaming, we must be alert to the historical context behind rules governing Native Americans, and the backdrop of power relations between federal and state governments and native peoples that continues to inform legislative change impinging directly on them.

THINKING ABOUT LAW AS A MECHANISM OF POWER

Many people believe law is an objective and neutral system of rules agreed upon and accepted through the processes of democracy. Laws, it is generally believed, are put into place for the protection and good of the general community. The truth is that law rarely fulfills that ideal. Law is and has always been a tool and technology of those in power. It is used to reinforce the social values and societal behaviors that most obviously benefit those who are in elite positions of economic, religious, or social control. Sally Merry, a legal anthropologist, notes that law works in a variety of ways:

> not just by the imposition of rules and punishments but also by the capacity to construct authoritative images of social relationships and actions, images that are symbolically powerful. Law provides a set of categories and frameworks through which the world is interpreted. Legal words and practices are cultural constructs which carry powerful meanings not just to those trained in law . . . but to the ordinary person as well. (Merry 1990:6)

In colonial regimes, it is easy to identify the cultural biases built into the legal system of the dominant colonial power. Law, in a variety of ways, was the formal mechanism and institutional frame through which governments oppressed and controlled indigenous peoples (see Williams 1990; Nader and Ou 1998; Fitzpatrick 2001). Of course, there are many varieties of imposition and reception of law in colonial territories. In some cases, such as in Africa (Mamdani 1996), this involved co-opting native chiefs and traditional procedures of arbitration and dispute resolution between local villages. In other cases, such as in Australia, the British declared the continent *terra nullius,* or vacant, and argued that no human being occupied the land before their arrival.[1] This argument was only possible if it was thought that Australian Aboriginals were less than human, with no physical presence on the land and certainly no legal system that had to be accommodated (Reynolds 1996). In all colonial occupations of foreign countries, be they in Australia, South Africa, Canada, India, Papua New Guinea, the Congo, or Algeria, law—the symbol of European superiority, individual property rights, and sovereign state authority—provided the justification and discourse of oppression. Law allowed social inequality to be based on racial and ethnic discrimination. A fascinating study on this topic is that by Lauren Benton, called *Law and Colonial Cultures: Legal Regimes in World History 1400–1900* (2002). In this study Benton outlines how local legal norms and traditions played a very significant role in shaping over time colonial legal regimes. And as I briefly discuss in the following text, anthropologists in the 19th century played a role in helping colonial regimes justify their unfair legal practices.

---

[1]This legal doctrine was also adopted by the United States to justify "discovery" and acquisition of Native American land in cases such as *Johnson v. M'Intosh,* 21 U.S. 543 (1823).

Today the colonial regimes of the 18th and 19th centuries have largely disappeared. However, in the United States, as elsewhere, those with the most power in society continue to have the most influence on law. In the early industrial period, industrialists of the 19th and 20th centuries such as Carnegie, Rockefeller, and Ford, who owned the railways and industrial plants that helped to make the United States so economically powerful, exerted sufficient power over legislative processes to ensure that laws regarding tax structures, liability suits, and employee benefits all worked in their favor against the powerless assembly-line factory workers. Today the U.S. legal system continues to make laws that affect people from a variety of economic and social backgrounds in different ways. The financial scandals revolving around companies such as Enron, Arthur Anderson, and Worldcom that erupted in 2002 once again indicate how much our current legal system favors protecting corporate enterprise, and not the interests of the middle- to lower-class American. The U.S. legal system allows these companies to squander the life savings and pension funds of thousands of people while company executives have, on the whole, been allowed to walk away absolutely free with enormous severance packages and payout deals. And even if some top executives have been found liable for illegal actions taken, these charges are insignificant compared to the ceaseless abuse of the legal system by corporate powers in general. In the words of Lois Capps, congresswoman and representative for California's 23rd district:

> The pattern of corporate irresponsibility demonstrated by Enron, Worldcom, Adelphia, and other companies is deeply disturbing. People in powerful positions committed unethical—if not illegal—acts that caused workers to lose their jobs, investors to lose their holdings and retirees to lose their pensions and retirement savings. There is no question that these executives must be held accountable and future corporate scandals prevented. (*Santa Barbara News-Press,* September 2, 2002)

A great deal has been written about the cultural and political biases built into laws and legal systems (see Darian-Smith 1999; Darian-Smith and Fitzpatrick 1999). These biases happen in all countries, including the United States, Australia, Mexico, China, and Iraq. It does not seem to matter whether a country claims to have a democratic, socialist, or communist legal system. All law reflects the political ideologies, social values, and norms of a given society, and concurrently helps to shape new cultural values and behaviors over time. We must be very careful not to assume that law is a neutral and value-free system of rules that we should all obey without question. Law reflects power and ideology, and the question we must always ask is, whose economic and/or political advantage is furthered when any new law is made? For the purposes of this study, the questions become: Whose interests are at stake in legal reform and legislative change surrounding Indian gaming, and what are the specific interests involved?

COLONIALISM IN THE 19TH CENTURY AND THE RESERVATION ERA

The goals underlying federal policies relating to Native Americans have changed over the centuries. Prior to the mid-1800s, Indians were seen as a direct threat to the safety of Europeans, and so federal goals related to their extermination or at least removal from all possible interactions with whites. But from the 19th century on, when it became apparent that Native Americans were not simply going to die out, the U.S. federal government started taking a different approach and advocated assimilation of Native Americans into mainstream society. Sincere, though misguided, efforts were made to make "them" more like "us." The most effective policy toward this end was "to gain legal control over the tribes through legislation" (O'Brien 1989:71). This meant reinterpreting the legal relationship between Indians and Euro-Americans that had existed since the time of "conquest and discovery." Unlike the British colonial regime in Australia, which deemed the continent empty and the Australian Aboriginal people to not exist, the government in North America deemed that Native Americans had occupied the land before the settlement and westward expansion of white colonists. This meant, at least technically, that colonists had to negotiate through legal treaties over landholdings and resources, since these officially belonged to Indian tribes. "In 1778, the United States government entered into its first treaty with the Indians—the Delaware tribe. In the course of the next century over six hundred treaties were made with tribes and nations" (Deloria and Lytle 1983:2–4). According to Howard Meredith, in his book entitled *Modern American Indian Tribal Government & Politics: An Interdisciplinary Study:*

> The relationships between American Indian tribes and the Untied States government have a common factor. The United States recognizes the Indian tribes as distinct, independent, political communities. As such the tribes are qualified to exercise powers of self-government, but not by virtue of any delegation of powers from federal government, rather it is by reason of their original tribal sovereignty. (Meredith 1993:18)

Treaties were made by tribal leaders with white settlers on the basis that Indians, not whites, owned the land (see Figure 2.3). Hence there was a general understanding that certain lands would be granted to settlers in exchange for promises that Indian lands and sovereign control over those lands would remain in Indian hands, and "would be protected by the United States forever" (Wilkinson 1993:29). It is important to appreciate that treaties were not a means by which whites gave Indians reservation lands, since these lands were deemed to be owned by tribes in the first place. Rather, under the original legal relationship established in the early colonial period, Indians had the contractual authority to give to whites some of their lands in exchange for the ongoing recognition and protection of their remaining sovereign territories. The act of creating treaties symbolized that "the federal government had acknowledged the tribes as distinct political communities with full authority and rights to manage their own affairs" (O'Brien 1989:71).

As white settlers increased in population, tribes were forced to move farther and farther westward. The violent use of the law, coupled with the decimation of the Native American populations, justified whites' acquisition of land on an enormous scale. Certainly some Native American tribes agreed under treaty to move from their homelands to new reservations. However, these agreements were not exactly voluntary; many tribes were forced to participate in an unjust legal system. "As in the past, the transfer of land went through the legal process of treaty making. And, as in the past, the whites bribed and tricked the Indian chiefs and in the end forced the chiefs to accept what they could not prevent" (Henretta et al. 1993:525). The result of the westward expansion by whites was that thousands of Indians were moved to the vast region west of the Mississippi designated by the federal government as the Unorganized Indian Territory (see Figure 2.4). The Cherokee, for instance, were

NEW YORK IN 1660.

Ian Darian-Smith

Figure 2.3 Peter Styvessant contracting with Indians, New York, 1660. Reprinted with special permission from Ian Darian-Smith.

forced to walk from their lands in Georgia to Oklahoma—a walk over hundreds of miles that became known as the "Trail of Tears" because of the appalling conditions to which the Native Americans were subjected.

"Indian Territory" was in theory protected for the sole use of tribes under the Indian Removal Act of 1830 because it was thought at the time that no whites would ever want to settle in the great desert landscape of what is now Oklahoma, Arkansas, and Kansas. Between 1832 and 1842, 19 tribes, which involved over 50,000 people, were relocated under duress to this territory. This was in effect the precursor to the reservation system.

GENERAL ALLOTMENT ACT (1887)

By the late 19th century it was clear that the lands originally designated as Indian Territory were in fact valuable for the ever-growing white population. In order to be able to settle lands earlier granted to tribes under the Removal Act and other treaties, the recognition of Indian sovereignty and respect for their policies of isolation on designated territories had to be changed. A new act called the General Allotment Act of 1887, commonly known as the Dawes Act, was passed. This was a legal manipulation of land rights in favor of white settlers. Under the act, Indian reservations were to be divided and redistributed to individual tribal members as their personal property. Heads of families received 160 acres, single people over 18 years received 80

Figure 2.4 Sioux Indians in covered wagons on the trail

acres, and all other tribal members received 40 acres. At first this seemed a generous federal plan, since it acknowledged the rights of individual Indians to plots of land and encouraged them to take up farming and agricultural practices in the same way as white settlers did. Land ownership of small farms by individual Native Americans was considered to be one means of aiding their assimilation into white society. However, in reality this act effectively removed a great deal of land from Native Americans. While Indians who were allotted land could receive U.S. citizenship, "with this provision there came a problem: as citizens, Indians would have to pay property taxes; but if they were unable to meet the assessments, they would be liable to lose their lands to the whites" (Dunn 1995:97). The result of the Dawes Act was that it conveniently provided the rationale for land removal from collective tribal communities. According to a commentary of the time in the *Saturday Evening Post:*

> In the eyes of the law the Indian originally held an anonymous position, neither citizen nor alien, and incapable of becoming a citizen; but the disabilities have been removed, and Indians are now enabled to leave their tribes or renounce the tribal system as a body, and become citizens. (December 25, 1897, cited in Beidler and Egge 2000:2)

The cost of becoming assimilated and becoming "real" American citizens was enormous for Native Americans. As the minority opinion on the Dawes Act stated in 1880:

> The real purpose of this bill is to get at the Indian lands and open them up to settlement. The provisions for the apparent benefit of the Indians are but the pretext to get at his lands and occupy them. . . . If this were done in the name of greed, it would be bad enough; but to do it in the name of humanity, and under the cloak of an ardent desire to promote the Indian's welfare by making him like ourselves where he will or not, is infinitely worse. (cited in O'Brien 1989:78)

Under the Dawes Act, individual Indians held land in their own right, leaving the remaining "leftover" lands to the federal government to be redistributed to white settlers, creating a checkerboard of Indian and non-Indian landholdings. This process proved disastrous for Indian tribes, culturally, politically, and economically. The concept of individual property rights disrupted the idea of community-based tribal lands, and personally owned farming plots represented a very alien existence for most Native Americans. Politically, the allotment process broke up traditional tribal governments and heralded their declining significance. Economically, huge parcels of land were lost to tribes and their land base was reduced from 140 million acres to 50 million over a period of 50 years.

According to Martin Charlot, son of Old Chariot, chief of the Flathead-Salish who occupied prime agricultural land in the Bitterroot Valley, Montana, in the late 1890s:

In the Bitterroot when my grandfather, Victor, was chief, we Salish started farming. The government told us to do it and we did. We had no equipment except the few things the [federal] agent gave us, such as harness and plows. We made fenceposts in the mountains and hauled them home by packing them on our horses. Then time went on and my grandfather died. My father, Charlot, became chief. . . . Everything was going along fine. We were making a good living and learning the White man's way. Then Garfield came to see us. He came to visit my father, for Charlot was the head man among the Salish. Garfield told my father that we would have to move out of the Bitterroot. . . .

"I am doing some farming," my father said. "I am getting good crops and my people and I are living as the agents and priests have taught us to do. I am not going to move."

"If you don't move you will be treated like a fish in dirty water," Garfield said.

"This is my home," my father answered. "By the 1855 treaty, we don't have to move. We will stay in Bitterroot." . . .

We tried to keep on farming, but Whites came in and homesteaded our land. We could not keep the little patches where we had fenced and had raised our crops. The wild game kept getting scarcer and scarcer. Nearly 20 years went by. We had no money or supplies from the government. . . . My father sent word that we would move. . . .But when we moved to the Jocko, things were not the way they were promised. Whatever we got we had to work for. There was no new machinery nor household stuff for those people who had left theirs behind. . . . We never got the cow and the calf apiece like we were promised. My father did not get his new house. . . . The men in the tribe did all that work digging ditches without getting much pay for it. After the irrigation system was in, many more people started farming. They were successful in farming on both sides of the Jocko River. In time, we even had a threshing machine. Just as we had done in the Bitterroot before the trouble began, we started helping each other out and got quite a bit of farming done. After the harvest, we took the grain to the flour mill and had it made up into flour for our winter provisions. The surplus grain we sold. All in all, we made a good living.

But those days didn't last either. Pretty soon, maybe in 15 years, engineers surveyed the reservation. When my father asked why they were doing it, they told him that the government was just making a survey to determine the acreage. But it wasn't long before we were allotted and the Whites moved in. Then, the government took hold of the irrigation system. They made it bigger, all right, but the Indians didn't get the water when they wanted it and needed it. Their crops burned up. Some of them went into debt. Pretty soon, most of them quit farming. The White man took everything. (Charlot 1991:270–271)

Needless to say, much of the reservation lands that were designated surplus and redistributed to whites was of better quality, with greater water and mineral resources. This inequity in land distribution further widened the gap between relatively rich white settlers and impoverished Indians who, often in complete desperation, had little choice but to sell what landholdings they held to white farmers and become underpaid employees of white ranch owners. The overall impact was devastating, as

Wilcomb Washburn, a leading expert on the impact of colonialism on Indian cultures, has noted:

> The blow was less economic than psychological and even spiritual. A way of life had been smashed; a value system destroyed. Indian poverty, ignorance, and ill health were the results. The admired order and the sense of community often observed in early Indian communities were replaced by the easily caricatured features of rootless, shiftless, drunken outcasts, so familiar to the reader of early twentieth-century newspapers. (Washburn 1995:75–76)

INDIAN REORGANIZATION ACT (1936)

Fortunately, the assimilation policies established under the Dawes Act were legally reversed under the Indian Reorganization Act of 1936 (IRA), which came to be known as the New Deal for Indians. This act was promoted by the federal Indian Commissioner John Collier, an anthropologist who had firsthand experience living with Pueblo Indians and was deeply committed to revitalizing Indian culture and sovereignty. With the help of Associate Solicitor Felix Cohen and President Roosevelt, Collier convinced those in Congress that the exploitation and degradation of most Indian peoples had to stop. The New Deal prevented the sale of reservations to white settlers and encouraged the establishment of new tribal governments and Indian self-management. The IRA represented shifting public attitudes toward Indian populations and, in some cases, a genuine desire to improve their terrible plight.

While well intended, the IRA did not fulfill its promise. The act was imposed with no input from tribes, and as a consequence "the tribal governments it created imposed an alien form of government on tribal cultures" that took the shape of specified constitutions (O'Brien 1989:82). According to Sharon O'Brien, a leading expert on Indian governance:

> Today about half of all tribes have IRA constitutions, all of which are, in general, very similar. A typical IRA constitution establishes a governing board, often called the tribal council. Unlike federal and state governments, most IRA constitutions do not provide for the separation of powers. The executive, legislative, and, in many instances, judicial functions are performed by the governing board. Council members are elected at large or by district by all voters. The chairperson and other officers who form the executive committee are members of the council, elected either by the people or by the council from among its membership. (O'Brien 1989:83)

O'Brien goes on to point out that a required secretarial approval clause in IRA constitutions undermines the intent to create self-sufficient independent tribal governments. The secretarial approval clause "empowers the secretary of the interior to approve or veto new tribal laws, to overrule certain tribal council actions, to call elections and settle election disputes, to oversee the tribes' economic affairs, to review the taxation of nonmembers, and to approve the hiring of legal counsel" (O'Brien 1989:83). In effect, this clause continued the domination of the federal government through the Bureau of Indian Affairs (BIA). The BIA was established in 1824 in order to cope with the increasing role played by the federal government in reservation life. The BIA was charged with acting as the guardian and overseer of all Native Americans affairs, and organized the selling to tribes of rations such as food, clothing, and other necessities. It also oversaw the education of Indian schoolchildren and administered reservation law enforcement officers. This paternalistic attitude toward

Indian peoples was damaging since it stripped tribes of confidence and the ability to manage their own internal relationships. But in practice, the situation was worse than many imagined, with the majority of BIA agents, largely ignorant of Indian culture, joining the Bureau to exploit their authority by setting up monopolies on supplies and selling goods at outrageously high prices to Indians on isolated reservations with no other options but to pay.

THE STATE OF CALIFORNIA AND ITS TREATMENT OF INDIAN POPULATIONS

In the wake of the annexation of California from Mexico in 1848 under the Hilgado Treaty, and the gold rush of 1848–1849 which brought an increasing immigration of white settlers to the west, California had sufficient population and political clout to become a U.S. state in 1850. Important to note is that "it entered the Union with a virulent anti-Indian policy" (O'Brien 1989:64). Death from introduced disease as well as open wars between whites and tribes in California took a huge toll on Indian populations. Even though California was originally one of the most densely popu-lated Indian regions with an estimated 150,000 inhabitants, by 1890 the state's Indian population had decreased to only 17,000, a 90 percent decline. Writes O'Brien:

> Hoping to reduce hostilities, the federal government negotiated a number of treaties with Indians in California in the 1850s. The tribes ceded half the state, reserving for themselves eight million acres in perpetuity. Under pressure from Californians, however, the Senate did not ratify the treaties, and the tribes lost all their lands. Not until the early 1900s were California tribes granted rights to some of their former lands. . . . (O'Brien 1989:63–64)

Given the extreme hostility toward Indian communities in California, in 1909 President Roosevelt established 117 small *rancherias* or reservations for Indian use. These reservations were inadequate in that they did not in any way compensate many tribes for lost lands and resources. Throughout the first half of the 20th century, there was open hostility toward native peoples and an unofficial policy of racism and denial of their poverty and lack of opportunities. Amidst continuing lack of sympa-thy toward native peoples, aggressive state lobbying of Congress brought about the passage of Public Law 280 in 1955 (see Goldberg 1996). This federal public law granted criminal jurisdiction over Indian lands to the state. The law was a landmark in that it overruled the long-established authority of the Bureau of Indian Affairs, the federal agency that up to that point had been solely responsible for native issues across the country. Public Law 280 also highlighted the increasing tensions between the overarching federal agency and the 50 state agencies in claiming jurisdictional control over Indian lands and Indian self-government. These tensions between fed-eral and state agencies over Indian affairs continue to this day, especially with regard to the regulation and control of Indian gaming and commercial ventures on officially designated reservation land. In Chapter 3 we discuss the tensions with regard to Indian gaming and casino operations in more detail.

THE BUREAU OF INDIAN AFFAIRS TODAY

While tension marks the federal and state legal battles over Indian gaming and its legal regulation and future, the Bureau of Indian Affairs (BIA) has increasingly come under attack for its historic mishandling of its bureaucratic processes. Almost all commentators on Indian issues and colonialism agree that such processes have been mishandled. The BIA has long held an unflattering reputation as the branch of federal government responsible for the exploitation and degradation of Indian peoples. According to Washburn:

> its tendency to self-aggrandizement has not only been carried on by deceiving or ignoring the Indian, but, on occasion, also by flouting the will of the Secretary of the Interior and of the Department's Solicitor who reviews Indian Bureau rulings. In part, the history of the Bureau of Indian Affairs reflects the normal process of bureaucratic growth; in part it reflects the antipathy or ignorance of the dominant white majority concerning the Indian minority. The combination of these two attributes has caused the Bureau to have achieved the unenviable reputation of being either hopeless or hateful. Few government bureaus have a less savory record. (Washburn 1995:208)

In recent years the unsavory reputation of the BIA has reached new heights. The Bureau is now officially accused of mishandling the multibillion dollar fund held in trust for over 300,000 Native Americans that was established at the time of the Dawes Act in 1887. The trust holds and distributes royalties raised for 54 million acres of land leased on behalf of Indians to commercial enterprises for drilling, grazing, mining, and logging. The fees are meant to be placed in trust funds and distributed on an annual basis to individual tribal members whose land is leased. However, it has become clear over the past decade that much of the money raised was stolen, misappropriated, or never collected. It is now estimated that more than $10 billion that should have gone to Indian landowners have been lost.

Elouise Cobell, a Blackfoot Indian who for over three decades has worked as the Blackfoot nation's treasurer, putting their chaotic accounts in order, is the dominant force behind the current investigations and lawsuit against the BIA. As the tribal treasurer:

> She began slogging through the books, such as they were, finding more questions than answers. Why, for instance, was the Blackfoot tribal trust drawing *negative* interest? How could this be when, by law, trust money must be invested by the government in the safest securities? Why was she seeing money leaving the tribal account when she was the only one authorized to write checks? When she raised the questions with the local BIA [office] from which much of the money flowed, the withering response was that she should learn to read a financial statement. (*Los Angeles Times Magazine,* July 2, 2002:17)

Frustrated but undeterred, Cobell starting talking with government representatives and members of Congress. She went to Washington, DC, at the invitation of Attorney General Janet Reno, but was again put off with empty promises. "It was the straw that broke the camel's back," Cobell says. In 1996, with the help of financial backing from the Otto Bremer Foundation of St. Paul, Minnesota, as well as a prestigious John D. MacArthur Foundation "genius award," Cobell worked with the Native American Rights Fund based in Boulder, Colorado, and filed a class-action lawsuit against the Interior and Treasury departments. The suit, with Cobell as the lead plaintiff, was made on behalf of a half million Native Americans, and accuses the two government agencies of failing to fulfill their fiduciary duties to manage the trust funds.

So far the findings in the case against the BIA point to corruption and chaos within the Bureau. The BIA has been unable to produce records to show how much

Indians have been paid since 1887. Many documents have disintegrated over time, and 162 boxes of relevant papers have been shredded since the trial began. Moreover, the Bureau's computer system was discovered to be so porous that hackers had set up trust accounts, forcing presiding U.S. District Judge Lamberth to shut down the system. In September 2002, Lamberth delivered a 276-page opinion in which he declared the Interior secretary, Gayle A. Norton, an "unfit" government representative. "The agency has indisputably proven to the court, Congress, and the individual Indian beneficiaries that it is either unwilling or unable to administer competently the . . . trust," Lamberth wrote. More significantly, there is evidence of fraud and intentional deceit. Lamberth's opinion continues, "The court is very disappointed that attorneys, particularly those that worked for the government, would engage in subterfuge" (*Los Angeles Times,* September 18, 2002). Despite the Bureau's obvious neglect and dishonesty, as of October 2002, not a single penny had been paid back to Indians for their loss of trust royalties. "The government is going to fight this no matter what, even if it's morally or ethically wrong," says Cobell. "That's a real crime in itself. They're in such denial, it's amazing. Congress needs to say no more money to fight this litigation" (*Los Angeles Times Magazine,* July 2, 2002:32).

The story about Cobell's fight to bring a legal action against the federal government is a story of an individual's bravery and courage in the face of open discrimination and ridicule. It is also the latest piece in the history of the treatment of Native Americans by the Bureau, which for over 100 years has openly exploited Indian lands and neglected its basic fiduciary duties to an impoverished minority. The current response of the government to refuse to right obvious wrongs is indicative of the continuing injustices and inequities that plague Indian and government relations. It remains to be seen whether the U.S. legal system will ultimately allow Native Americans to win their case or whether it will, as in the past, be used to serve the dominant society's best interests and deny any wrongdoing despite the clear and copious amount of evidence to the contrary.

JURISDICTION AND SOVEREIGNTY IN INDIAN COUNTRY

In the late 19th century it was widely thought by both social scientists and the general American population that Indian peoples were less intelligent than white people, and consequently had a lower capacity for rational thought. This general opinion also supported the idea that Native Americans could not possess legal systems and sophisticated rules of governance. Such a line of reasoning conveniently suited 19th-century desires to conquer and possess Indian lands, and provided the rationale for paternalistic policies that treated Indians like children who were incapable of managing themselves. President Thomas Jefferson, who epitomized basic 19th-century enlightenment values, espoused that Indians had to be legally managed by whites because of their basic inferiority, and ordered the explorers Lewis and Clark to gather ethnographic information about the tribes they met as they set out on their journey west toward the Pacific in 1804. Jefferson believed that reliable scientific information about indigenous tribes would make it easier to assimilate them into white society and ultimately to extinguish Indian land titles. Scientific knowledge served the legal system and the dominant cultural values and social priorities of the time, just as it continues to do to this day.

The Dawes Act of 1887 and the later Indian Reorganization Act of 1936 represent shifting social values held by whites toward native peoples. From the open exploitation of tribes and the blatant removal of reservation lands, to the more progressive hope for native self-government and revitalization of their cultures, attitudes toward native peoples boil down to how much legal control, or sovereignty rights, to grant to Native Americans. Because a legal system symbolizes a sophisticated cultural and political structure, the amount of recognition given to the right of indigenous communities to sovereign control over their own people and territories functions, in a sense, as a barometer that measures the temper of our dominant cultural values toward Indians.

Indian country is the term used to refer to land within Indian reservations, as well as land outside reservation boundaries owned by Indians but technically held in trust for them by the federal government (see the previous section). Having legal jurisdiction refers to whether a government, be it tribal or state, can make and enforce its own laws with regard to controlling its own territory or the people who occupy that territory. Disagreements over what is "Indian country" and who has jurisdiction over that land have been at the heart of over 200 years of fierce legal battles that continue to this day between Indians and non-Indians in regard to the issue of native legal sovereignty (see Deloria 1996; Deloria and Lytle 1998; Deloria and Wilkins 1999).

Before white settlement in the United States, Indian tribes had full jurisdiction and full control over their lands. They were in effect independent sovereign nations, capable of managing and governing through traditional Indian law their own peoples, crimes, land disputes, and relations with other tribes. However, some early anthropologists such as Daniel Brinton, who became professor of ethnology at the Academy of Natural Sciences of Philadelphia in 1884, and wrote a regular column titled "Current Notes in Anthropology" in the journal *Science,* claimed that Native Americans did not have sophisticated legal systems and certainly no institutional structure equivalent to modern nation-states. He argued that for this reason Native Americans could not be considered on a par with white colonists. Brinton and other scholars such as Herbert Spencer and John Wesley Powell based such arguments on "scientific" facts and helped to confirm the prevailing 19th-century assumptions that Indians were "savages" with barbaric methods of internal governance (see Baker 1998:33, 40). These social scientists established, largely through the powerful use of scientific language, a social evolutionary model that placed Indians well below Europeans in terms of their capacity for intellectual thought and their level of legal knowledge.

Within the United States, people such as Samuel George Morton, a student of medicine from Philadelphia, provided "scientific evidence" of Indian inferiority. In Morton's 1839 study, the *Crania Americana,* Morton measured the capacity of 144 Indian skulls from across the continent and compared those measurements with others taken from the skulls of Caucasians. Tinkering with the statistical results, he concluded that the brain size, and thus the intellectual capacity, of European descendants was far larger than the brain size of native peoples. This led Morton to write about native peoples: "The structure of the mind appears to be different from that of the white man, nor can the two harmonize in the social relations except on the most limited scale." Furthermore, Indians "are not only averse to the restraints of education, but on the most part are incapable of a continued process of rationing on abstract subjects" (cited in Gould 1996:89; see also Baker 1998).

Morton was certainly not alone in his endorsement of a social evolutionary model that claimed Native Americans and African Americans were inferior based on their racial characteristics and genetic makeup. In the 1890s, Frederick Starr, an anthropologist at the University of Chicago, argued that minority peoples were predisposed to criminal activity, given their barbaric moral values and inherent savage behaviors (Baker 1998:54–61). Through public exhibitions and popular journals, academic attitudes about racial hierarchy were disseminated into the wider community. The 1893 World's Colombian Exposition in Chicago featured a presentation of the "low and degrading phases of Indian Life." In the words of Emma Sickles, a protestor at the time, "[E]very effort has been put forth to make the Indian exhibit mislead the American people. It has been used to work up sentiment against the Indian by showing that he is either savage or can be educated only by government agencies" (cited in Baker 1998:60). According to anthropologist Lee Baker:

> Turn-of-the-century anthropological science not only responded to but also intensified the significance of U.S. racial categories. . . . When anthropology became an academic discipline [in the late 19th century], there were two areas of popular culture in which its scientific authority became particularly important: world's fairs and widely circulated magazines. Both were suffused with images and narratives that affirmed ideas about the racial inferiority of people of color. (Baker 1998:54–55)

Since the 1970s, the American Indian Movement (AIM) has helped foster a growing awareness among non-Indian populations about indigenous rights to self-government and self-determination in the United States. In academic circles, anthropologists no longer believe in a 19th-century racial hierarchy and now fully appreciate and acknowledge that tribes have always had traditional legal structures and a concept of legal order. Contemporary anthropologists argue that although Indian laws may not be equivalent to or operate like the U.S. legal code, they are nonetheless valid in their own right (see Gooding and Darian-Smith 2001). That being said, it is still not entirely clear what Indian sovereignty means. Today, in certain instances, tribes have concurrent or shared jurisdiction with federal and state governments. "In other situations, depending on the state, the type of crime [criminal or civil], and the race of the individual involved [Indian or non-Indian], state or federal law may take precedence" (O'Brien 1989:207). As Table 2.1 illustrates, depending on whether an action is a minor civil offense (called a misdemeanor) or a major crime (involving such acts as assault, rape, or murder), and depending on the ethnic designation of both the accused and the victim of the crime, different agencies have jurisdictional authority to investigate the case, and different courts will ultimately decide what happens. As Table 2.1 shows, the result is a highly complicated jurisdictional maze that creates enormous difficulties for predicting with certainty how cases occurring on reservation land will proceed and who will have authority over them.

INDIAN GAMING AND THE CONTINUING ISSUE OF LEGAL SOVEREIGNTY

Laws regarding Indian gaming are as complicated as other laws in terms of jurisdiction. Do federal, state, or tribal jurisdictions have the power to dictate what happens on California Indian reservations? At the heart of the legal cases and conflicts are the

TABLE 2.1 Jurisdictional Authority of Various Agencies

	Accused	**Victims**	**Agency in Charge**	**Court Deciding Case**
Misdemeanors	Non-Indian	Non-Indian	State or county	State
	Non-Indian	Indian	FBI	Federal
	Indian	Non-Indian	FBI	Federal
	Indian	Indian	Tribal	Tribal
Major Crimes	Non-Indian	Non-Indian	State or county	Federal
	Non-Indian	Indian	FBI or BIA	Federal
	Indian	Non-Indian	FBI or BIA	Federal
	Indian	Indian	Tribal	Tribal

questions of Indian sovereignty and whether tribes have the right to establish and run casino operations in their own territories, even if the laws of the states in which the reservations are located prohibit casino gaming. Law continues to be one of the most significant sites through which Indian and non-Indian relations are debated, negotiated, and validated. Law helps to establish and reinforce cultural boundaries between people. At the same time, it defines allowable behaviors and "official" attitudes that perpetuate social, political, and economic differences between dominant and minority populations. In order to understand and analyze what is going on in the United States regarding Indian and non-Indian relations we need to look beyond the obvious, and not lose sight of the historical context of Indian law and its ongoing inequities and political ramifications.

SUGGESTED FURTHER READING

Baker, Lee D. (1998) *From Savage to Negro: Anthropology and the Construction of Race 1896–1954.* Berkeley: University of California Press.

Benton, Lauren (2002) *Law and Colonial Cultures: Legal Regimes in World History 1400–1900.* Cambridge: Cambridge University Press.

Carrillo, Jo (ed) (1998) *Readings in American Indian Law: Recalling the Rhythm of Survival.* Philadelphia: Temple University Press.

Darian-Smith, Eve (forthcoming) *Challenges to State Law: Surveying Local Attitudes about Indian Gaming in Santa Barbara County, California.*

Darian-Smith, Eve and Peter Fitzpatrick (eds) (1999) *Laws of the Postcolonial.* Ann Arbor: University of Michigan Press.

Deloria, Vine Jr. (1996) Reserving to Themselves: Treaties and the Powers of Indian Tribes. *Arizona Law Review* Vol. 38(3):963–997.

Deloria, Vine Jr. and Clifford M. Lytle (1998) (2nd ed) *The Nations Within: The Past and Future of American Indian Sovereignty.* Austin: University of Texas Press.

Deloria, Vine Jr. and David E. Wilkins (1999) *Tribes, Treaties, and Constitutional Tribulations.* Austin: University of Texas Press.

Dunn, John M. (1995) *The Relocation of the North American Indian.* San Diego: Lucent Books.

Fitzpatrick, Peter (2001) *Modernism and the Grounds of Law.* Cambridge: Cambridge University Press.

Gooding, Susan and Eve Darian-Smith (eds) (2001) Putting Law in Its Place in Native North America; Symposium. *Political and Legal Anthropology Review (PoLAR)* Vol. 24(2).

Jaimes, M. Annette (ed) (1992) *The State of Native America: Genocide, Colonization, and Resistance.* Boston: South End Press.

O'Brien, Sharon (1989) *American Indian Tribal Governments.* Norman: University of Oklahoma Press.

Peckham, Howard and Charles Gibson (1969) *Attitudes of Colonial Powers toward the American Indian*. Salt Lake City: University of Utah Press.

Pommersheim, Frank (1995) *Braid of Feathers: American Indian Law and Contemporary Tribal Life*. Berkeley: University of California Press.

St. Germain, Jill (2001) *Indian Treaty-Making Policy in the United States and Canada, 1867–1877*. Lincoln and London: University of Nebraska Press.

Washburn, Wilcomb E. (1995) (2nd ed) *Red Man's Land/White Man's Law: The Past and Present Status of the American Indian*. Norman and London: University of Oklahoma Press.

Wilkins, David E. (2002) *American Indian Politics and the American Political System*. Cumnor Hill: Rowman and Littlefield.

Wilkins, David E. (1997) *American Indian Sovereignty and the U.S. Supreme Court: The Masking of Justice*. Austin: University of Texas Press.

Wilkinson, Charles F. (1987) *American Indians, Time and the Law*. New Haven and London: Yale University Press.

Williams, Robert A. (1990) *The American Indian in Western Legal Thought: The Discourses of Conquest*. New York and Oxford: Oxford University Press.

Wunder, John R. (ed) (1996) *Native American Law and Colonialism, Before 1776 to 1903*. New York and London: Garland.

3/The History
of Indian Gaming
in the United States

INTRODUCTION

Gambling, or gaming, as it is more commonly known today in commercial circles, has become one of the biggest boom industries of the 21st century. Gaming includes a variety of activities, such as state lotteries, horse and dog tracks, card rooms, betting on sports events, casinos, and a burgeoning new trade in Internet betting. In 1962, North Americans spent about $2 billion on gambling, but this figure rose rapidly: By 2000, the country was betting $866 billion (see Table 3.1). From this $866 billion, the commercial take was approximately 10 percent, which means that the gambling industry gained about $70 billion in 2000. Given that the amount of money spent on all tickets to movies, plays, concerts, live performances, and sports events in the year 2000 totaled only $22 billion, North Americans spent three times as much on gaming in 2000 as on all other forms of entertainment combined. This is a surprisingly enormous sum. "State lotteries and casinos are the two most popular formats, accounting for most of the growth. Lotteries have sprung up everywhere since New Hampshire began the trend in 1963. Casinos, in contrast, remained confined to Nevada deserts for nearly half a century, but have proliferated rapidly since 1988" (Lambert 2002:34).

This chapter briefly outlines the history of casinos in the United States and contrasts that history with the more recent history of Indian casinos that have become firmly established in number and popularity since the early 1980s. It is important to realize that Indian casinos, which have caused a great deal of controversy and in some cases open hostility by politicians, commercial gaming operators, and local communities, raise only 17 percent of all legal gambling revenue. In contrast, commercial non-Indian casinos raise approximately 43 percent. In short, Indian casinos represent a small fraction of the total gaming industry (see Figure 3.1).

Arguments against Indian gaming on the basis that it encourages immorality, crime, and deviancy and that it promotes pathological behavior and gambling addictions must be qualified. A good percentage of the annual gambling revenue in the United States is sponsored through and run by state governments, highlighting the hypocrisy and shallowness of negative opinions about Indian gaming. I am not suggesting that gambling is an innocent pursuit and in no way connected to promoting

TABLE 3.1 TOTAL ESTIMATED SUMS
WAGERED IN THE UNITED STATES

1962	$2 billion
1976	$18 billion
1985	$80 billion
1993	$400 billion
2000	$866 billion

Source: Data compiled by Paul Weiler, 1998 and 2000.

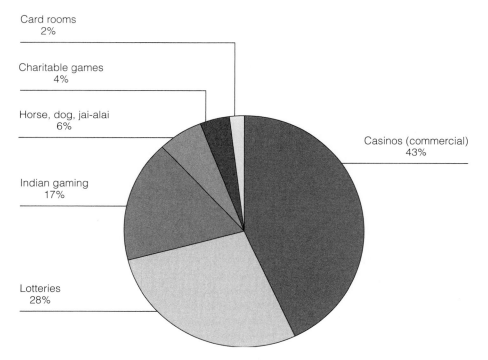

Card rooms
2%

Charitable games
4%

Horse, dog, jai-alai
6%

Casinos (commercial)
43%

Indian gaming
17%

Lotteries
28%

Figure 3.1 Legal gambling revenue: Percent of gross revenues by sector, 2000. Source: American Gaming Association, 2000.

particular activities and behaviors that are not healthy for our general society. But a moral stance against gambling should be directed at all formats in which it appears, and not specifically at Indian casinos on reservations, which are no more or less problematic than the local 7-Eleven store selling lottery tickets or the glitzy, popular, and family-oriented casinos on the strip in Las Vegas.

GAMING IN LAS VEGAS AND OTHER NON-INDIAN CASINOS

In 1864, amid the bitter desert landscape of land politics, mining prospects, and ranch herding, Nevada became an officially recognized state. Nevada's statehood served the interests of President Lincoln, who needed the state's taxes from mining revenues to help pay for his Civil War effort in the battle against slavery. There was a feeling at the time, which prevailed into the 20th century, that Nevada came into existence solely through the manipulation of the federal legal system and that it was in a sense a sham state, a pawn in the power politics of the nation's leaders. According to one Yale professor, William H. Brewer, who opposed statehood for Nevada, "I see no elements here to make a state. It has mines of some marvelous richness, but it has nothing else, nothing to call people here to live and find homes. . . . The climate is bad, water is bad, land a desert, and the population floating" (cited in Thomson 1999:196).

Interestingly, gambling was originally forbidden in Nevada—"it captivates and ensnares the young, blunts all the moral sensibilities and ends in utter ruin," warned the governor of Nevada in the 1860s (cited in Thomson 1999:35–36). However, despite dominant moral sensibilities, between 1869 and 1910 gambling was legal in Nevada and tolerated by most people. This changed in 1910, as state officials attempted to earn credibility in the east by presenting Nevada as a region of law and order, the effects of which made gambling illegal and forced it to go underground. This new law had only a minor impact, however, since in Nevada it was never difficult to gamble or drink, despite prohibition laws that outlawed alcohol consumption. The puritanical moral tone that gripped the country in the early part of the 20th century changed with the stock bust of 1929 and the onset of the Great Depression. Nevada suffered greatly under the bleak economic climate. In a desperate bid to raise revenues and take advantage of the influx of construction crews that flooded Las Vegas to build the Hoover Dam, the state introduced two pieces of legislation. The first reduced the waiting period for divorce from three months to six weeks, and the second permitted casino gambling. Both pieces of legislation attracted transitory visitors to the state and encouraged spending and tourism.

Between 1930 and 1940 Las Vegas's population rose steeply from a few thousand to more than 8,000 residents. This rise was further sustained when in 1937 the Union Pacific railroad struck an artesian well that guaranteed water for the booming city and electricity from the dam fed by the Colorado River. People from Los Angeles started visiting Las Vegas for weekend getaways to see the wonders of the Hoover Dam and to take advantage of the growing casino industry. While most of the gambling halls at this time were still on the rough side and harked back to frontier cowboy days, in 1931 Tony Cornero opened the Meadows Club to attract a different kind of risk taker. The Meadows Club was a supper club and dance hall, with chandeliers, tablecloths, and men in white jackets and bow ties. Following the success of the Meadows Club, other upscale clubs were established, such as the Golden Nugget, the Pioneer, the El Dorado, and the El Cortez in what today is known in Las Vegas as Old Town. Throughout the late 1940s, the 1950s, and the 1960s, Las Vegas enjoyed a sort of dubious notoriety, with links to gangsters and organized crime, Hollywood movie stars and big spenders, and a flourishing national music and entertainment industry. As the only state in the country to allow casino activities, Nevada monopolized high-stakes gambling and took advantage of its flourishing tourist industry. (For more history of Las Vegas, see Moehring 2000.)

Las Vegas's dominance in the field of gambling changed in 1978 when an economic recession convinced New Jersey voters to approve a referendum to make casinos legal in Atlantic City. No longer was it necessary to make the long trek to Nevada. Atlantic City attracted large numbers of people on day visits from the surrounding big cities of Philadelphia and New York. Quickly the success of Atlantic

City caught on, and between 1989 and 1998, nine more states (including Mississippi, Connecticut, Iowa, and Minnesota) legalized casino gambling. By 2002, 429 non-Indian casinos were legally operating in 11 states.

Apart from the current impact of the Internet and the new wave of nonstop gambling and "instant-win" lottery tickets and slot machines, one of the most important changes to the gaming industry in recent years is in the public's perception of it. Not long ago, many people considered gambling to be deviant behavior, associated with crime, addiction, and other black-market vices such as prostitution and drugs. Today, the general public accepts gambling as part of everyday life in the United States. According to a national Gallup poll in 1999, 63 percent of the public approves of gambling. As long as it is done in moderation, 75 percent find it equivalent to going to a movie or sporting event. Only 26 percent find it morally wrong and think it should be stopped. Helping this shift in public opinion has been state governmental promotion of gambling in the form of state lotteries, and church endorsement of bingo games. Historically the church and state bitterly opposed gambling of any sort, but Howard Shaffer, director of Harvard Medical School's Division on Addictions, notes, "They are now the two greatest proponents of gambling" (Lambert 2002:35).

This shift in public opinion from viewing gaming as a vice to seeing it as legitimate entertainment is dramatically evidenced in the architectural changes on the Las Vegas strip over the past 10 to 15 years, with the building or revamping of hotel-casinos such as New York–New York, the Luxor pyramid, Caesars Palace, Bellagio, Paris Las Vegas, and the Venetian (see Figures 3.2 and 3.3). As its promotional brochures proudly attest, Las Vegas is like no other town. In 2000 Las Vegas had over 35 million visitors. Eleven of the 12 largest hotels in the world are located there, some with over 5,000 rooms. Billed as the biggest entertainment and nightspot capital of the world, housing some 30 casinos, expanding with the nation's fastest metropolitan growth rate, and accommodating over 1.5 million permanent residents, Las Vegas is a unique phenomenon.

Las Vegas represents a hub of entertainment for predominantly middle-class Anglo-Americans and foreign tourists, combining historical theme parks with roller-coaster–fun plazas and the orchestrated magic of Disneyland. No longer a center of adult-only pleasure, Las Vegas has become the "place" for the whole family. In the words of Ada Louise Huxtable, a theorist of American architecture:

> Since gambling has been renamed gaming (another triumph of still another uniquely American phenomenon, public relations), and thus cleansed of all pejorative connotations and rendered euphemistically harmless, it has emerged at the top of the list of America's favorite pastimes. Las Vegas may have begun as a thoroughly adult, mob headquarters off-limits to minors; [but] today places like Las Vegas and Atlantic City . . . are being touted as family vacation spots. It has finally all come together: the lunar theatrical landscape of the Strip and the casino hotels, the amusement park and the shopping mall, themed and prefabricated, available as a packaged vacation for all. (Huxtable 1997:78–79)

Las Vegas keeps a tenacious grip on its imagery of a fun-filled adventure land, despite the undercurrents of reality that periodically wash up on the shores of this desert oasis, such as the 1997 brutal murder of a 7-year-old girl in the toilets of the Primadonna resort on the California/Nevada border, and the gang-style slaying of rap singer Tupac Shakur on the central Las Vegas strip. The ugly images of city living—unemployed people, drug and gambling addiction, prostitution, labor

Eve Darian-Smith

Figure 3.2 New York–New York hotel-casino in Las Vegas, Nevada

exploitation, and substandard homes and hospitals—are necessarily pushed aside. Las Vegas relies on its advertising to create the illusion of a place where fortunes are lost and won, romance is guaranteed, second-rate Broadway shows abound, and cheap buffet dinners of steak and lobster are legendary.

WHAT IS INDIAN GAMING?

In contrast to the glitz and commercialism of places such as Las Vegas and Atlantic City, gaming (or gambling) has long been a tradition among Native American peoples. Originally used as part of tribal ceremonies and rituals, gaming was practiced in a variety of forms well before the arrival of Europeans in North America. With colonial contact, many early chroniclers observed the high stakes and terrible consequences of some gaming practices without appreciating the deeply symbolic meanings and religious undertones that informed these rituals (see Figure 3.4). One colonial report in 1872 remarked that among the Kailtas of California, the losers of gambling wagers "frequently slashed themselves from the ankles to the knees in

Eve Darian-Smith

Figure 3.3 Luxor casino in Las Vegas, Nevada

crisscrossed strokes with bits of flint and glass to appease whichever bad spirit was preventing their luck" (Culin, cited in Gabriel 1996:9). Church leaders in California missions were determined to force Indians to abandon their games, known as "heathen worship" (Gabriel 1996:9). The non-Indian populations failed to appreciate the significance of gambling practices among California tribes, as well as the accompanying gambling myths revolving around mythological animal kingdoms and characters such as Coyote, Prairie Falcon, Meadow Lark, Gopher, and Rabbit (Gabriel 1996:40). Coyote is one of the most recurrent characters to appear among most Native American groups. Though often presented as the trickiest of tricksters, and at times even as evil, Coyote is an ambiguous figure who can change sides and states, and who often supports both losers and winners in gambling matches.

Despite the deep mythological and symbolic meanings associated with gambling among Native Americans, it was not until the 19th century that early white observers of Indian culture, including anthropologists Frank Hamilton Cushing (1857–1900), Stewart Culin (1858–1929), and Lewis Henry Morgan (1818–1881), appreciated the connection between gambling and religion. For Native Americans, gaming is a supremely sacred activity, tied up with narratives and myths about social behavior and competitive interaction between tribes. The luck involved in winning and losing is very much linked to ideas of morality, sanctity, and the will of supreme deities or gods. In 1907 Stewart Culin wrote an 846-page volume, *Games of North American Indians,* which was published by the Smithsonian's Bureau of American Ethnology. This expansive volume was the culmination of 14 years of work and was one of many such publications produced by a number of non-Indian academics recording Native American cultural practices that focused on ritualized gaming and oral traditions evoking notions of luck and chance. (For a fascinating history of Indian games and ritual, see Gabriel 1996:1–30.)

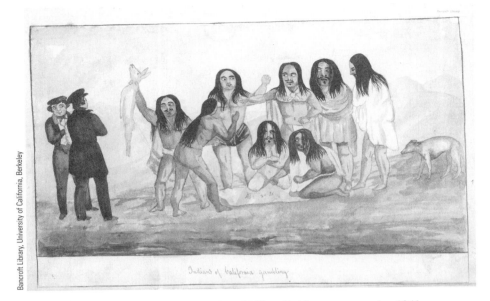

Indians of California Gambling

Bancroft Library, University of California, Berkeley

Figure 3.4 Indians of California Gambling, *William H. Meyers, watercolor, 1841*

For many Native Americans today, gambling, as it was in the past, is part of everyday life and the ongoing religious and symbolic meanings that infuse daily decisions and practices. Gambling is not so obviously connected with ideas of immorality and deviance, as it so often is in Western societies where a dominant Judeo-Christian moral code often views gambling as immoral. In contrast to many Native Americans, for the dominant white population in the United States, there remains a residue of unease about gaming and its connection with pathological addiction and exploitation of those incapable of self-control and restraint. For Native American communities, the lessons learned from such behavior inform complex traditions and myths. Instead of thinking that the state or church should control such gambling behavior, as the dominant non-Indian population claims, for many Native Americans the lessons learned from winning and losing, which often involve the overcoming of temptation and adversity, are regarded as an important part of personal growth and community experience. These lessons are passed down through myths and stories from generation to generation. In other words, many present-day Native Americans have a very different relationship to gambling than that experienced by the general population. This makes the establishment of casinos on reservation land, and the economic success of some of these casinos, less problematic for the majority of Native American peoples than it may be for some whites because gaming does not hold the same moral connotations. Casino operations are a source of revenue, to be viewed as a short-term economic venture. Casinos are solely a means to make profits and to provide opportunities for investment in new resources and commercial practices such as tourism and retail during the coming decades.

Today, Indian gaming refers to formalized gambling operations on tribal reservations that are very similar to those found in places such as Las Vegas and Atlantic

City. Gaming takes a variety of forms, ranging from the more modest Class I and Class II kinds of games (such as bingo, lotto, pull tabs, and card games) through Class III gaming, which has caused the most controversy and includes blackjack, craps, slot machines, and roulette. These casino-style games involve betting "against the house," and not surprisingly, they are the most profitable. Reservations that offer such games compete directly with places such as Atlantic City and Las Vegas in attracting potential gamblers; hence, they have caused the most vocal opposition and political protest from Atlantic City casino owners and people such as Donald Trump.

HISTORY OF INDIAN CASINOS IN THE UNITED STATES

Indian casinos, or tribal casinos, have a shorter but more controversial history than nontribal casinos (see Eadington 1998; Mason 2000; Mullis and Kamper 2000; Lew and Van Otten 1998; Mezey 1996; Symposium 1997). In 1979 the Seminole tribe in Florida opened a high-stakes bingo parlor, and other tribes quickly followed suit. Despite bitter opposition by some state governments and a great deal of political pressure, by 1999 over 150 tribes in 24 different states had opened high-stakes casino and bingo operations on their reservations. However, this group represents only about one-third of the 558 federally recognized tribes in the country, and of those tribes with casinos, a meager 22 generate more than half of all Indian gaming revenues. (For answers to frequently asked questions about Indian gaming, see Appendix A.)

Although some Indian casinos and bingo halls have been successful, such as Oregon's Spirit Mountain Casino which is the number one tourist attraction in the state, many tribal casinos have not made significant profits, and some have even failed economically. One of the primary reasons for failure is geographic isolation, as reservations are usually far from city centers and a sustainable clientele. For example, the "tribes of the Greater Sioux Nation, with thousands of members in North and South Dakota, run about a dozen gambling halls but generate comparatively little in the way of revenue because of the tribes' stark isolation" (*Boston Globe,* December 11, 2000). A modest Indian bingo hall is described in detail by Louise Erdrich, a renowned Native American novelist and member of the Turtle Mountain Band of Chippewa, in her novel *The Bingo Palace:*

> My place of employment is an all-purpose warehouse containing an area for gambling that Lyman hopes to enlarge, a bingo floor that converts to a dance area, and a bar, and there are even a few older makes of video games blinking dimly against the wall. . . . From outside, my place of work is a factorylike Quonset hut—aqua and black—one big half-cylinder of false hope that sits off the highway between here and Hoopdance. By day, the place looks shabby and raw—a rutted dirt parking lot bounds the rippled tin walls. Bare and glittering with broken glass, the wide expanse is pocked by deep holes. The Pabst [beer] sign hangs crooked and the flat wooden door sags as if it was shoved shut in too many faces, against hard fists. But you can't see dents in the walls or rips or litter once darkness falls. Then, because the palace is decked out with bands of Christmas tree lights and traveling neon disks that wink and flicker, it comes at you across the flat dim land like a Disney setup, like a circus show, a spaceship, a constellation that's collapsed. . . . But nobody notices how it looks after nine o'clock. (Erdrich 1994:40–41)

Each state has specific laws relating to Indian gaming within its state borders. In California, laws surrounding gambling are very complicated. As Bill Eadington, director of the Institute for the Study of Gambling and Commercial Gaming at the University of Nevada, has stated, "California's gaming scene is far more political than any jurisdiction in the world" (Mccoy n.d.). The regulation of Indian gaming represents a constant friction between state and federal jurisdictions as each seeks to control what each maintains is legally its domain. Historically, as noted earlier, the federal Bureau of Indian Affairs has governed all matters pertaining to Native Americans, but this arena of federalism has come under extreme pressure and challenges from individual states keen to regulate the activities within their own territorial borders. As an example, *California v. Cabazon Band of Mission Indians*, 480 U.S. 202, 207 (1987), held that California law may only be applied to Indian reservations located in the state primarily with the approval of Congress:

> The Court has consistently recognized that Indian tribes retain "attributes of sovereignty over both their members and their territory," *United States v. Mazurie*, 419 U.S. 544, 557 (1975), and that "tribal sovereignty is dependent upon, and subordinate to, only the Federal Government, not the States," *Washington v. Confederated Tribes of Colville Indian Reservation*, 447 U.S. 134, 154 (1980). It is clear, however, that state laws may be applied to tribal Indians on their reservations if Congress has expressly so provided. . . .

The Indian Gaming Regulatory Act of 1988 (IGRA) was introduced in response to the confusion about federal and state jurisdictional control over reservation casinos. The goal of the IGRA was to regulate Indian gaming operations as well as to provide some federal protection for tribes from state governments, which in many cases tried to curb Indian operations. In order to facilitate federal oversight of tribal casinos and enforce the IGRA, Congress established the National Indian Gaming Commission. Federal law allows tribes to set up bingo and a few other games on Indian reservations. When tribes want to introduce Las Vegas–style gaming or Class III gaming operations with high stakes, federal law mandates that individual tribes must negotiate agreements or compacts with state agencies. In most cases this has proven to be very difficult, with some states objecting to Indian casinos on moral grounds, and other states being influenced by the powerful lobby groups of Las Vegas and Atlantic City non-Indian casino owners, who are anxious not to lose their monopolies on high-stakes games. Even when tribes have been able to secure a compact, it comes at a price, since a tribe entering into a tribal-state compact concedes some of its sovereign authority over its peoples and lands to the state (Harvey 2000:25).

In contrast to the glamour of the enormous casino-hotels built or revamped in Las Vegas in the latter part of the 20th century, many Indian casinos are more modest in physical appearance and financial ambition. Still, some tribal casinos are moving toward full tourist operations like those in Las Vegas—hotels with shopping and outlet complexes, luxury accommodations, fancy restaurants, and a variety of family-oriented vacation attractions. One of the largest and most profitable of all Indian casinos is the Foxwoods Resort Casino in eastern Connecticut, which is owned and operated by the Mashantucket Pequot tribe. The government of Connecticut originally refused to allow the casino to be developed but eventually agreed to allow it when the Pequot tribe contracted to give the state 25 percent of its annual gross income (approximately $100 million annually). Even with this cut taken by the state, the casino has made sufficient profits that the tribe has been able to buy back some of its original landholdings, as well as provide its resident members with full health, safety, and educational services.

The financial success of the Foxwoods Resort Casino is not the norm for Indian casinos. However, more and more Indian casinos, both in California and in other states, are deliberately setting out to mimic what one finds in Las Vegas and Atlantic City, creating large tourist and commercial ventures and resorts. According to Michael Lombardi, a tribal gaming consultant and former general manager of the Chumash Casino in California:

> Before passage of the measure [Propositions 5 and 1A; see next section], Native American casinos operated in a legal never-never land. More often than not, they were confined to Spartan structures whose only allure was betting. . . . Tribes didn't know if they were going to be open from day to day. . . . Proposition 1A's assurance of legality brought Californian Native American bands a new economic viability. Today's lenders, including Bank of America and Wells Fargo, are opening their vaults for unprecedented financing of new resorts. . . . (*Los Angeles Times,* November 22, 2002)

HISTORY OF INDIAN GAMING IN CALIFORNIA AND PROPOSITIONS 5 AND 1A

Proposition 5 was an initiative put before California voters in November 1998, and later reaffirmed by Proposition 1A in March 2000 (see Mullis and Kamper 2000). What appeared to be a nonissue for California voters turned into a national spectacle that consumed a total of over $92 million in advertising and media propaganda, more than any other proposition in California history. Very simply, the proposition advocated that Indian people have the right to operate "Las Vegas–style gambling" on their reservations, and the state had no right to intervene, despite the fact that such new electronic forms of betting and slot machines are not allowed on non–Indian-owned California land.

Proposition 5 did not initially attract a great deal of pubic concern. Historically, California voters have been largely uninterested in Indian reservations, which are primarily governed by federal law. Hence, both the California Republicans and Democrats originally anticipated that Proposition 5 would not attract much public attention. Given the general history of public disinterest in Indian affairs and the relative lack of concern over the morality of gambling, the escalation of political and media hype over Proposition 5 and its passing by a 63 percent majority took a great deal of the California voting public by surprise. This escalation can be explained in part by the enormous economic profits at stake. To give the reader an idea of the figures involved, in California alone tribal gambling brought in $1.4 billion in total revenue in 1998. This partly explains why the opposition to Proposition 5, led by the former Republican governor of California Pete Wilson, spent $29 million in advertising campaigns. Nevada casino operators and card room, racetrack, and labor organizations, fearful that their profits would be diminished with Indian casino competition, largely financed this campaign. Those supporting Proposition 5 raised $63.2 million, surprisingly over twice as much as the opposition. Most of the funds came from a handful of wealthy Indian tribes in Riverside and San Bernardino counties, advocating for what they presented as "the right for Californian Indians to govern themselves on their own lands."

At first glance, the battle over Proposition 5 could be interpreted as a battle over who will get what percentage of the future gaming profits in the American southwest. The conflict, in other words, could be reduced to a contest similar to that of Microsoft and Apple competing for future speculation on the computer market. This interpretation, however, overlooks a whole range of historical continuities and cultural subjectivities that inform and underlie the bitterness and acceleration of the Proposition 5 conflict. From the perspective of many Native American Indians, November 3, 1998, was a triumphant day, with Proposition 5 being voted in by a 63 percent majority. As stated by George Forman, a San Francisco attorney involved in the initiative, Proposition 5 was "a watershed event." According to Forman, "The Indian tribes could never have qualified a measure for the ballot even five years ago, much less beat the largest and best-funded opposition in the country. . . . There's no way to overestimate the significance of what has just happened. Never in American history have so many people expressed themselves in such a positive way toward Indian tribes and tribal self-determination" (*Union-Tribune,* November 27, 1998; see also Maullin 1999). According to Viejas tribal chair Anthony Pico, "This was a real affirmation. The voters of California have said, 'Yes, you're welcome to be included in our family of governments, of economics, of real citizenship'" (*Union-Tribune,* November 27, 1998).

In material terms, the success of Proposition 5 represents real change for many Native Americans living on impoverished reservation lands. With limited forms of income, Native American Indians continue to represent the lowest socioeconomic community within the United States with a 31 percent poverty rate. As a minority group, they also have the highest rates of unemployment and health problems, suicide, and alcohol addiction (see Hill 1994). In the past few years, this image of impoverishment has slowly been changing with the introduction of tribal gaming. According to the San Francisco district attorney Terence Hallinan, "I know gambling can be a problem, and it needs some regulation, but an exception for tribal casinos is an opportunity to make some money for tribes who have no other realistic money-making opportunities on the horizon" (*San Francisco Bay Guardian*, September 30, 1998:21). Catherine Saubel is a Cahuilla elder and chair of the Los Angeles Coyotes Indian band who lives on a remote reservation that only in 1998 had electricity and telephone services installed, paid for by funds provided by the county's three gaming tribes. Said Saubel, "We're trying to live like everybody else. . . . We still don't have a lot of things other people have. . . . All through these years, since the invaders came into our lands, we've never had justice. . . . Now we have a little justice when the people of California voted for 5" (*Union-Tribune,* November 27, 1998).

As discussed in earlier chapters, the Native American population is not monolithic or homogenous, any more than is the dominant Anglo-Saxon population in the United States. One of the negative consequences of the public endorsement for tribal control over their own land is an increasing level of bitterness and anger between tribes with casinos and those without. There are also tension and bitterness among Native American "traditionalists" and "modernists" who differ in their opinions about the success of gaming and the potential harm it causes their cultural heritage, customs, and identities (see Fenelon 2000). In some cases, long-standing tribal members are angry at the surge in the numbers of people claiming Native American ancestry for entitlement to casino dividends. In the state of Connecticut, where in 1992 the Mashantucket Pequots opened the Foxwoods Resort Casino and in 1996 the

Mohegans opened the Mohegan Sun Casino, the Indian population in the state has doubled. "Money is the greatest attraction in the world," said Ralph Sturges, long-time chief of the casino-owning Mohegan tribe in Connecticut. Of course, proving "authentic" tribal ancestry is not that simple in many cases; often it involves "blood quantum" requirements that call for proof of Indian ancestry in the form of specified blood quotas (see Washburn 1995:163–168; Perry 1995; Dan 1998). For instance, the Catawba tribe of South Carolina, the Paiutes of Nevada, and the Tigua of Texas have all debated the rules of blood quantum and tribal membership in the past year.

Despite the new cleavages and divisions occurring across Native American communities, those few tribes involved in successful casino operations see that their strengthening economic position is translating into a newfound cultural confidence and pride on reservations. Although only 2 to 3 percent of tribes with casinos are highly successful, the financial spin-off is gradually filtering down among a wider range of Indian communities. More and more tribes are building houses, schools, and community centers, as well as casinos and resorts. In a few cases, such as the 30,000-square-foot museum currently being planned by the Cahuilla Indians in Palm Springs, native peoples are entering the lucrative artifacts market and attempting to buy back their cultural heritage (*Las Vegas Sun,* March 15, 1999). For instance, the Pechanga Band of Luiseno Indians, which operates a casino near Temecula in southern California, vied for the rights to display rare Indian artifacts currently housed in the Southwest Museum in Mount Washington, near downtown Los Angeles. The Pechanga's competitor was the Autry Museum of Western Heritage, founded by the late cowboy singer and actor Gene Autry and his wife Jackie. The preliminary bid by the Pechanga band, which was to pay the museum $750,000 to $1.3 million yearly, caused some alarm among conservative groups that were dismayed by the Indians' association with casino operations. But as noted by Douglas Sharon, director of San Diego's Museum of Man, "Museums have a long track record of going to corporations. Casinos are another corporate presence" (*San Diego Union Tribune,* October 23, 2001). And according to Duane Champagne, director of the American Indian Studies Center at UCLA, "The gambling is a means to an end. These people are native and this is about preserving their community and culture" (*San Diego Union Tribune,* October 23, 2001). While the Pechanga bid to merge with the Southwest Museum ultimately failed (*Los Angeles Times,* December 11, 2002), profits from Indian casinos are indeed going toward the construction of reservation museums. One of the most notable of these is the Pequot Museum, funded by the Foxwoods Resort Casino, which has proven to be a significant tourist attraction in its own right.

On a more overtly political level, the wealthier and more powerful tribes are demanding a role in California's governmental procedures (see *Bee Capitol Bureau,* January 24, 1999). In late March 1999, the inaugural meeting of the Democratic Party's Native American Indian Caucus was held in Palm Springs. The caucus drew hundreds of delegates with the specific aim of increasing the presence of Indian political representatives. This new tribal activism has also fueled political activity beyond established party politics. In March of 1999, Anthony Pico, chair of the Viejas Casino and Turf Club, delivered what may have been the first "state of the tribe" address in California. This highly symbolic act intentionally mirrored addresses given by representatives of state and federal governments, and was designed so that the tribe could publicly declare "its place at the table of governments" (*Union-Tribune,* March 23, 1999). According to Pico, "tribes are governments. . . . [W]e are not an extinct people or a stagnant culture." This is vividly demonstrated by the tribe's ownership of the largest and most prosperous tribal casino in California, along with its new adjoining $35 million factory-outlet center, and its major shareholding interest in the Borrego Springs Bank. Says Pico, "Yes, the entrepreneurial spirit is alive and flourishing for the Viejas Band of Kumeyaay Indians. For that we honor our elders and our ancestors before them, who were not satisfied with dependency on the United States government. They believed we would once again find the means to chart our own economic course as an Indian nation" (*Union-Tribune,* March 23, 1999).

There are 108 federally recognized tribes in California. As of January 2002, 50 of these tribes had gaming ventures on their land. Under federal law, these tribes are required to maintain their own reservations, as well as contribute a percentage of their earnings to a Special Distribution Fund that redistributes monies to neighboring communities affected by the casino. These tribes are also required to share a percentage of their profits with tribes without casinos under the Revenue Sharing Trust Fund, which has saved the federal government millions of dollars in recent years. So whether directly or indirectly involved in gaming activities, all tribes, to varying degrees, are improving the quality of life for their tribal members.

THE "NEW BUFFALO" AND THE FUTURE OF NATIVE AMERICAN INDEPENDENCE

Indian gaming is often referred to by the pro–Indian gaming movement as the "new buffalo." This reference is to the huge herds of buffalo that up until the 19th century roamed the central plains, providing for many tribes a source of economic and social survival (Figure 3.5). During the westward expansion of the American frontier, buffalo were systematically wiped out for their hide and meat, as well as for sport. With the introduction of rifles and horses, and motivated by the bounties paid for bison carcasses, Native Americans often contributed to the mass killings of buffalo. The building of railroads also contributed to the devastation of the vast bison herds, with hunting from trains widely advertised as a form of recreation. By 1889 the vast northern and southern herds, which once consisted of millions of bison, were destroyed by settlers and industrialists, leaving less than 600 buffalo in the United States. Native Americans, who were often treated like animals, were also killed or rounded up and placed on faraway reservations. According to Art Raymond, a Plains Indian:

> The buffalo went through the same kind of experience our people went through. There were millions and millions of buffalo. And gradually, through the years, the buffalo herds were pushed westward, and grew fewer and fewer in number. Our people went though the same kind of experience. General Sheridan said that in order to get to the root of the problem we must exterminate Indian men, women and children. That's what he said. And later on, in order to help bring about the extermination, the word was put out by the military to kill off all the buffalo, to encourage the slaughter of the buffalo at every turn. (interview for a documentary film titled *Sacred Buffalo People,* http://redeyvideo.com/buffalo.htm)

Native Americans, denied their economic base and resources in the form of the buffalo, as well as their complex kinship networks and dependence upon the land, were plagued by poverty, disease, and illiteracy throughout the 19th and 20th centuries. High mortality rates prevailed. The 1990 and 2000 U.S. Census both revealed that Native Americans continue to have the highest poverty and unemployment rates

Western History Collections, University of Oklahoma Libraries, Campbell #1659.

Figure 3.5 Herd of buffalo in South Dakota, circa 1930s

in the United States. To this day, the life expectancy of Native Americans is approximately 50 years, contrasted with the non-Indian average of 78 years.

Against this bleak background, Indian gaming represents, for the first time, economic security and independence from federal and state government agencies that have historically controlled and maintained Native American populations. Of course, casino operations on reservations are not always enormously successful. For instance, four tribes in north San Diego County have had to scale back their plans to build $100 million–plus resort hotels, convention centers, and themed tourist attractions. The scaling back is due in part to the tribes' geographical remoteness from major urban populations, to their close proximity to each other and a possible saturation of the market, and to economic belt-tightening after the events of September 11 (*Santa Barbara News-Press January 5, 2002*).

However, on those few reservations where gaming has been relatively successful, the proceeds have vastly improved housing, health, education, and self-esteem, and in some cases have resulted in the financing of cultural centers and museums detailing the local unique histories of specific tribes. In a profound sense, many tribes are seeking to revive their customs and traditions, and revitalize their sense of unique cultural identities and affiliations. Gaming on reservations allows Native Americans, for the first time, to envisage a real possibility of taking charge of their own futures and well-being. As noted by Indian historian Donald L. Fixico, Native Americans are now facing the need to both preserve their traditions and identity and, at the same time, participate in the business world. They are doing this by:

> taking the bingo money and, for example in the Creek Nation [in Oklahoma], putting it into their own hospital; . . . they have a staff with Indian nurses and Indian doctors. They're taking that money and putting it into scholarship money for college aid. So

whatever the BIA gives you up to a certain scholarship amount, then the tribe will help to fund that as well. They've reinvested that money back into the tribe, into various programs, not business programs but types of social services to help their own people: a tribal elderly program, a feeding program, a nursing program, and all kinds of things like that, in addition to putting much of the money into kinds of war chests. Because . . . the Bingo operations of the tribes in Oklahoma have banded together into a coalition and the state government attorneys are restudying tribal sovereignty to tax bingo tribes. It's going to be a war of economics. (Fixico 1991:424–425)

In the 21st century, Native American gaming has undoubtedly become a "war of economics" in Oklahoma and many other U.S. states. This war is bitter and extremely controversial. Many tribal leaders and tribal members do not fully approve of gaming as an economic strategy and are keen to diversify their profits into other economic ventures. However, at the moment gaming provides the only real option for native peoples to gain legal and political sovereignty, assert their unique cultural identities, and secure treatment as social equals to their non-native fellow citizens. It is no wonder that many still consider gaming operations, or the "new buffalo," to be the single hope for a better future.

CHALLENGING THE CONSTITUTION, REDEFINING THE LAW

Self-sufficiency and sovereign independence for native peoples was one vision never imagined or endorsed by the federal government and original supporters of the Bureau of Indian Affairs. This vision of self-sufficiency, which includes Native Americans having their own laws and system of governance entirely separate from those of the United States, presents a strong challenge to the prevailing ideal of a hegemonic and singular American legal system and culture. Ironically, the increasing demands by Native Americans for gaming rights build upon 19th-century colonial law that placed native peoples on distant reservations, out of sight and out of mind from modern society. The historical arguments put forward by the U.S. federal government, which were designed to isolate and disempower Native Americans, are now being turned on their head. These very same arguments are being used to justify why Native Americans on reservations should continue to have different laws applied to them, only this time these laws operate in favor of tribes by providing exceptions to the rules on gaming that govern the wider state. In this way, Indian gaming presents new directions in Native Americans' ability to build independent arenas of economic and political significance within the wider authority of the United States.

Casino operations on reservations represent the most important challenge to enduring legal discrimination against Indian peoples by both federal and state governments. In a sense, the future of Indian legal sovereignty, which rests on whether a tribe is allowed to control what goes on within its bounded territories, is being decided currently in the state of California over the issue of Indian gaming. As the largest state in the United States in terms of geographic size and population, California represents the state with potentially the highest profit margin from casino operations. Native Americans are already exercising significant influence on state and federal politics. As a result, Indian gaming in California is attracting a great deal of attention. What unfolds in California will point to the future of Native Americans and their legal sovereignty across the whole of the country.

California (and more generally, the West) also performs a highly symbolic role in the popular U.S. imagination. Philip Burnham, a scholar and journalist who has lived and taught for several years on the Rosebud Sioux Reservation in South Dakota, sums up the significance of the West in thinking about the future of Native Americans:

> Since the creation of the reservations in the mid-nineteenth century, the West is where the vast majority of Indian trust land resides. Land is seminal to our understanding of Indian history, and in recognition of the claims that remain to be settled in U.S. courts, of the future of Indian Country as well. The land—by implication, the West—is not a settled thing. . . . The native has literally "returned." (Burnham 1996:202–203)

This sense of native peoples "returning" to take a rightful place in the cultural, political, and economic institutions of the United States underscores the significance of the Propositions 5 and 1A victories in California. These propositions allow Native Americans to run casinos on their own lands, and these victories reverse a long historical trend, dating back to earliest colonial times, of white domination and exploitation of native peoples in the name of law, order, and justice. Propositions 5 and 1A represent a new era of Indian and non-Indian relations in California that finally acknowledges past injustices and takes an interest in the enduring future of Native Americans. In defending their rights to establish casinos and profit from gaming on reservations, Native Americans have to deal increasingly with, and be listened to by, politicians, policy makers, lawyers, and businesspeople. Both Democrat and Republican leaders can no longer entirely ignore or avoid the needs of Native Americans who are, little by little, making substantial financial contributions in support of specific party platforms.

In July 2002, U.S. District Court Judge David F. Levi of Sacramento rejected a lawsuit filed by four Bay Area card rooms led by Artichoke Joe's in San Reno. The card rooms objected to Propositions 5 and 1A, and the granting of a monopoly on Las Vegas–style gaming in California to Native Americans. They sued Governor Gray Davis, who had issued compacts with tribes allowing them to set up casinos on reservations, and they sued the Department of the Interior which had signed the compacts. Noted Judge Levi, "The grant of an economic monopoly to any group presents serious questions that should cause careful consideration and hesitation." However, he concluded, "Where the political branches and the people of California have adopted a policy that does not violate either federal law or the U.S. constitution, that policy is entitled to prevail" (*Los Angeles Times,* July 30, 2002).

The ruling has been crucial in creating legal stability and allowing tribes to attract financial investment and long-term security that will help, in turn, finance new services and facilities on reservations. "We're thrilled that the judge upheld the overwhelming will of the electorate," declared Mark Macarro, chair of the Pechanga Band of Luiseno Mission Indians, which runs a successful casino in Palm Springs. "One of the frustrating things for the tribes has been an inability to plan and know where they stand," noted Jerome Levine, an attorney representing the tribes in the case. "It has impaired their ability to get financing." Professor I. Nelson Rose of Whittier Law School in Costa Mesa has predicted that if Judge Levi's decision is affirmed on appeal, the ruling could have an impact on other states, such as Arizona and Connecticut, where tribes have rights to operate gambling facilities that are broader than those held by non-Indians (*LA Times,* July 30, 2002). In short, the ruling represents a milestone with significant and profound implications for long-term legal recognition of all Native American sovereignty rights. The ruling is the logical outcome of the notion of sovereignty, and it redefines the legal meaning of sovereignty for indigenous peoples in the United States.

By challenging state authorities and having native peoples' sovereign rights confirmed by the U.S. federal court, Native Americans in California and across the nation are beginning to experience the emergence of a new era in which they may finally be allowed to govern themselves and manage their own lives. There is a new feeling of confidence and purpose among some of the tribes with casinos as these people are for the first time getting a chance at the "American dream," and are now able to provide health, education, and social services for their members. It is important not to idealize or romanticize the motivations of Native Americans in operating casinos. Native Americans are interested in making money as much as anyone else. But what this newfound wealth does is open windows of opportunities that have never been available to them before, and so it represents a great deal more in social, cultural, and political terms than simply being able to buy a fast car or expensive house. There is a growing sense of pride, as reflected in a moving thank-you message from Indian leaders to the people of California in the wake of the U.S. District Court's upholding of Proposition 1A as being constitutional under federal law:

Indian leaders thank Californians:

The U.S. District Court of the Eastern District of California has found Proposition 1A to be constitutionally sound and rejected a lawsuit by a small group of California card room operators. California Indian communities are deeply gratified to see the U.S. District Court uphold the overwhelming mandate of California voters for Indian self-reliance. We are grateful to the millions of Californians and thousands of organizations that gave us their support and commitment. With this legal challenge behind us, California Indian tribes can continue on our path to self-reliance.

The lawsuit, which challenged Proposition 1A, was filed by a disgruntled handful of card room operators against the state of California. It sought to expand gaming beyond state and federal limits and to destroy the progress that tribes and the state have made after a decade of conflict. The lawsuit was a desperate measure to attempt to overrule federal law and Supreme Court decisions that have consistently upheld the constitutional status of tribal governments—not racial groups—to use gaming as a form of economic development.

The court decision affirms the rights of tribes as governments to offer gaming and found Proposition 1A to be consistent with federal gaming law. The overwhelming majority of Californians want to see the limited and regulated tribal gaming authorized in Proposition 1A continue uninterrupted.

The Governor, Lieutenant Governor, California State Assembly and Senate, State Attorney General, California Federation of Labor, taxpayer groups, chambers of commerce, law enforcement, religious and ethnic leaders joined together to support Proposition 1A. The tribal-state gaming agreements, made possible by the passage of Proposition 1A were signed by 61 tribal governments and subsequently approved by the Department of the Interior.

Thanks to Proposition 1A, Indian gaming is transforming the lives of California Indians and is allowing us to provide better health-care, housing and education for our people. We continue to be grateful to the millions of Californians and thousands of organizations that gave us their support and commitment.

SUGGESTED FURTHER READING

Darian-Smith, Eve (2002) Savage Capitalists: Law and Politics Surrounding Indian Casino Operations in California. *Studies in Law, Politics and Society* Vol. 26:109–140.

Eadington, William R. (ed) (1998) *Indian Gaming and the Law.* Reno: University of Nevada.

Gabriel, Kathryn (1996) *Gambler Way: Indian Gaming in Mythology, History and American Archeology in North America.* Boulder: Johnson Books.

Lew, Alan A. and George A. Van Otten (eds) (1998) *Tourism and Gaming on American Indian Lands.* New York: Cognizant Communication Corporation.

Mason, W. Dale (2000) *Indian Gaming: Tribal Sovereignty and American Politics.* Norman: University of Oklahoma Press.

Mezey, Naomi (1996) The Distribution of Wealth, Sovereignty, and Culture through Indian Gaming. *Stanford Law Review* Vol. 48(3):711–737.

Moehring, Eugene P. (2000) *Resort City in the Sunbelt: Las Vegas, 1930–2000.* Reno and Las Vegas: University of Nevada Press.

Mullis, Angela and David Kamper (eds) (2000) *Indian Gaming: Who Wins?* UCLA American Indian Studies Center, Los Angeles: Contemporary American Indian Issues Series No. 9.

Symposium: Indian Gaming. (1997, Spring) *Arizona State Law Journal* Vol. 29(1).

Thomson, David (1999) *In Nevada: The Land, the People, God and Chance.* New York: Alfred A. Knopf.

4/The Chumash Indian Casino Expansion Project

INTRODUCTION

The city of Santa Barbara, on the southern coast of California, is a beautiful resort town about an hour and a half drive north from Los Angeles. Its striking quasi-Spanish architecture, sweeping beaches, overflowing red bougainvilleas, luxury cars, expensive restaurants, and splendid sunny weather make it one of the most desirable places to live in the United States, and one of the most popular tourist destinations for Americans and foreigners. Near the coast of Santa Barbara is the low mountain range of the Santa Ynez Valley Here boutique wineries owned by people such as Fess Parker, the B-grade actor who played Davey Crocket and Daniel Boone in the 1960s, provide wonderful distractions of good food and excellent wine for visitors. Set against a rolling landscape of attractive farms, green golf courses, and elite pony clubs, it should come as no surprise that many long-term residents refer to the region familiarly as "Reagan Country." Since the 1920s and 1930s Santa Barbara and its surrounding county region have been favorite destinations for retired conservative politicians, as well as Hollywood and pop star refugees such as Michael Jackson, Bo Derek, Cheryl Ladd, Oprah Winfrey, Whoopi Goldberg, and John Cleese, just to name a few.

Santa Barbara residents rarely think about it, but beneath the city's beauty and luxury lies a dark historical past that involves oppressive Catholicism, exploitation, rape, disease, and murder. The city's colonial heritage includes the exploitation and abuse of Chumash Indians, the local indigenous communities of the region, who throughout the late 18th and early 19th centuries were treated like slaves by the Spanish missionaries, Mexican revolutionaries, and Anglo-American settlers. The Indians, forced off their land and made to give up their culture and complex tribal organization, were put to work for the Catholic mission and helped sustain the church's power over the region until the 1830s. While the secularization of the church in 1833 supposedly granted Chumash Indians freedom and liberty, by that time their kinship networks and traditional way of life had been completely disrupted. As Bruce Miller, a specialist on Chumash notes:

Secularization didn't change the demands on the Chumash: the Presidio [garrisoned fort] at Santa Barbara still insisted on work without recompense. By 1839 there were 246 Indians living at the Santa Barbara Mission and its vicinity. Thus, in six decades, the space of a single lifetime, the Chumash nation whose territory stretched over 7,000 square miles and whose people numbered many thousands had been reduced to near extinction. Culturally and spiritually they had very nearly ceased to exist. (Miller 1988:35)

In 1994, after centuries of poverty and legal and social discrimination, the Chumash Indians opened a casino on their reservation in the Santa Ynez Valley, about 50 miles inland from coastal Santa Barbara (see Figure 4.1). Despite initial skepticism by many local residents on the coast as well as surrounding the reservation, the casino has been extremely successful. This economic success led to plans to expand the facility, and in July 2002, amidst extreme local opposition, the tribe began building a new casino complex that includes a resort hotel, administration building, and larger casino floor.

This chapter is about local responses to the Chumash Casino expansion plans. By exploring why some local residents and politicians in Santa Barbara County were antagonistic to the plans, we can begin to appreciate some of the deeper cultural biases and enduring stereotypes that permeate non-Indian discussions about Native Americans, including charges that Indians are "lawless" and don't pay taxes. Exploring a local case such as the Chumash tribe's casino expansion plans, and how local communities have responded to it, is crucial for a grounded approach to the issue of Indian gaming more generally. This chapter also balances theoretical and abstract discussions about Native Americans in contemporary U.S. culture with a concrete event that is currently unfolding. We know from the last chapter that the wider California voting population supports Indian gaming by a significant majority. National polls also show that across the United States, about 65 percent of the entire population agrees that Indian gaming and Indian casinos should be allowed. Against this large national and state support, local community responses point to a very different opinion. In the case of the Chumash Casino and other proposed casinos across California, it appears that people living in close proximity to reservations are not as pleased with the idea of Indian casinos as national and state polls otherwise indicate. In September 2002, as a supplement to my personal interviews and observations, I conducted a phone survey with the help of the Survey Center at the University of California, Santa Barbara. This survey interviewed 731 people and showed overwhelming opposition to the Chumash Casino among residents living in close proximity to the reservation in comparison to residents living in the northern and southern parts of the Santa Barbara County (see Darian-Smith forthcoming). This chapter attempts to untangle the reasons.

A BRIEF HISTORY OF THE CHUMASH INDIANS

Historically, the Chumash Indians occupied a wide stretch of territory from San Luis Obispo to Malibu Canyon along the Pacific coast, and inland about 80 miles to the western edge of the San Joaquin Valley. They also occupied some of the islands in the Santa Barbara Channel. While population estimates vary, it is believed that up to

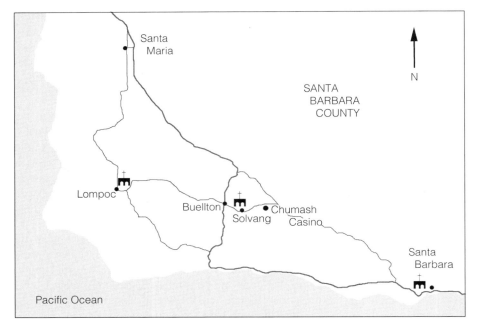

Figure 4.1 Map of Santa Barbara County, California

25,000 lived in permanent villages mostly along the coast, and that this population developed over a period of 7,000 to 10,000 years. Judging from artifacts and cave art, the Chumash were a highly sophisticated community of approximately 150 villages (called *rancherias* by the Spanish), with chiefdoms, a monetary economy, craft specialization, and a heavily involved barter and trade network with other indigenous groups within California and beyond.

The Portugese explorer, Juan Rodríquez Cabrillo, sailing under the Spanish flag, first contacted the Chumash in 1542 as he entered the Santa Barbara Channel on his way north from Mexico. Cabrillo was sailing up the coast of New Spain looking for an alternative route to China. Touching down along the coast at present-day Ventura and Carpinteria, he was greeted by friendly Chumash who supplied him with fish and water. In *The Diary of the Voyage,* Cabrillo noted:

> All these towns are between the first *rancheria, Las Canoas,* which they call *Xucu,* and this point (five miles west of Point Goleta). They are in very good country with fine plains, and many groves and savannahs. The Indians go dressed in skins . . . and they wore their hair very long and tied up with long strings interwoven in the hair; to the strings they attached gewgaws of flint, bone and wood. . . . They say that in the interior there are many *rancherias.* (cited in Miller 1988:18)

Over the next 200 years, there was very little contact between Europeans and Chumash apart from an exchange between Sebastian Vizcáino in 1602, and then Don Gaspar de Portolá in 1769. Portolá's assignment was to declare Spain's claim on *Neuva California* and establish permanent settlements in the area. In this venture, Portolá came into contact with numerous Chumash Indians, who again were hospitable toward him and his 65 men. According to Friar Crespí, who was traveling with the men, "the Indians were quite friendly but they played weird flutes all night and kept us awake" (cited in Miller 1988:21). Portolá's expedition traveled north to San Francisco Bay before returning south to San Diego. On a second voyage north, Portolá again stumbled on Monterey Bay, which had originally been sited by Vizcáino, and there he was quickly joined by Father Junipero Serra.

MISSIONS AND SLAVERY

Father Junipero Serra was born on the island of Majorca off the coast of Spain in 1713, and studied at the University of Majorca before arriving in Mexico in 1749. He was a man of extreme conviction in his commitment to convert the California Indians to Catholicism and make them productive citizens of the Spanish colonial state. In the effort to convert the "heathen savages," the Franciscan father helped establish five missions in Chumash territory: San Luis Obispo (1772), San Buenventura (1782), Santa Barbara (1786), La Purísima Concepción (1787), and Santa Ynez (1808). These five missions formed part of a trail of twenty-one missions along a route that wound north from San Diego along the California coast up to San Francisco Bay. The missions were a deliberate colonizing strategy to establish permanent settlements and harness control through creating a system of dependency and submission for the indigenous populations of the area.

Although Serra died in 1784 without seeing the building of the Santa Barbara Mission, his successor, Padre Presidente Fermin Lasuen, took over construction in 1786. Local Chumash from a nearby village were quickly relocated to help build an aqueduct and establish agricultural crops. Many eventually were converted to Catholicism for economic reasons or by more oppressive forces that included the exploitation and rape of women and children. By 1788, there were 428 recorded Chumash converts living on the outskirts of the mission in makeshift campsites. They were told to abandon their traditional religious beliefs and social practices, and in return they were taught European skills such as sewing and spinning, metal forging, woodworking, animal husbandry, and tilemaking. The mission system depended entirely on the Chumash who were in effect considered slave labor. Not only did the Chumash build and maintain the mission, but they were also farmed out to local settlers and soldiers as a labor force for which the mission was paid in return. Without the Chumash, the colonial Catholic system would have certainly failed. As the historian Bruce Miller notes:

> By 1799, at the Santa Barbara Mission the Chumash had built a large church, six chapels that stood alongside, a granary, a jail, a quadrangle surrounding the entire mission area with walls eight and one half feet tall and measuring 3,300 feet in length, and nineteen adobe walled, tile roofed houses nearby for themselves. In addition, thirty-one houses of the same type were built on the site of their old village to accommodate the new converts. By the end of the year the Death Register at the Santa Barbara Mission had 736 entries. (Miller 1988:30–31)

The mission population of Chumash Indians reached its peak in 1805 when it was recorded that 5,602 Chumash were living at the five missions. However, due to disease, neglect, and the repercussions of a revolt in 1824, this population steadily declined over the following 30 years. "By 1832, the last year for which accurate statistics are available, the mission Chumash population had been reduced to 1,182 people" (Walker and Johnson 1994:111). Two years later in 1834, the Mexican government, which had earlier declared its independence from Spain in 1824, decided to secularize the missions and take hold of the huge landholdings of the Catholic Church. The Chumash were told they were free to leave the missions and take up land for themselves. However, this change of law did not help many of the remaining Indians who were left without sufficient skills or internal kinship networks to survive the transition to become individual landowners. With the California gold rush in 1848, and the annihilation of 50,000 Indians throughout the whole state in a matter of a few years, the Chumash were essentially crushed. "By the time of the first California state census in 1852, the Chumash had been reduced to fewer than 600 people" (Walker and Johnson 1994:111).

THE CHUMASH BAND OF MISSION INDIANS TODAY

Currently there are about 5,000 people who identify themselves as Chumash. These people make up a number of different Chumash tribes, but only the Iniseno band, often called the Chumash Band of Mission Indians, from the Santa Ynez Valley have been recognized under federal law. This recognition meant that the Santa Ynez tribe was given a small 127-acre parcel of land in 1901 for a reservation very close to the old Santa Ynez Mission. Today about 150 Chumash live on this reservation. The remaining bands, including the Barbareno, Canalino, and Obispeno, while numbering somewhere between 4,000 and 5,000 people, have no official recognition and no reservation, a fact that has caused some tension between the groups, especially in recent years.

As the casino has become more and more lucrative, some Chumash have claimed that they are being cheated out of gaming profits. In order to benefit from the casino proceeds, one must prove a blood quantum of one-quarter Chumash, though there is talk of reducing this to one-eighth. In any case, the old tensions that centered around who has or does not have federal recognition are currently revitalized and escalated in Santa Barbara County, and across the whole of the United States, mostly in response to the success of Indian casinos. Ed Ruiz, a local Santa Barbara contractor and member of a coastal, nonrecognized Chumash tribe, told me that the casino has torn apart the indigenous peoples of the region, created enormous conflicts and bitterness, and elicited threats of legal action by nonrecognized Chumash against those who live on the reservation. According to Ruiz, the reservation Indians are not about to share their casino profits anytime soon, and it was no surprise that many of them voted Republican (interview September 2002).

The most recent outburst of intratribal tension erupted on the steps of the Santa Barbara Mission at the opening of the annual "Old Spanish Days" Fiesta celebration on Wednesday, July 31, 2002 (see Figures 4.2 and 4.3). James Navarro, an 18-year-old Chumash tribal member, disrupted Santa Ynez tribal dancers in protest against Chumash participation in the celebration, and specifically the dancers' use of Apache music which employs drums and not the traditional Chumash clapstick. Navarro was dragged off the stage by police. Two of the dancers were Navarro's uncle and cousin, which indicates the depth of feeling and bitterness between families and relations.

The Old Spanish Days incident encapsulates the ongoing tensions among all Chumash people over whether to participate in a celebration that symbolizes the

Mitch Robles

Figure 4.2 The Old Spanish Days celebration at the Santa Barbara Mission

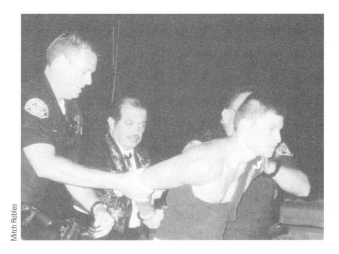

Mitch Robles

Figure 4.3 James Navarro, a member of the Chumash tribe, arrested on July 31, 2002, at the Santa Barbara Mission

oppression and enslavement of Indians under the mission system. It is hard to deny the strange and profound irony of Indians celebrating the heyday of Spanish control. Escalating the tension has been the donation of $20,000 given to the Fiesta organizers by the Santa Ynez Mission Indians as part of their proceeds from the casino. Notes Stephen Franco, former vice chair of the Coastal Band of the Chumash Nation:

> Participating in something as devastating to our ancestors as this is very much a slap in the face. . . . Let's wake people up and tell them what Fiesta is really about. Its roots are the California Chumash Indian and it's turned into Old Spanish Days. It should be Old Chumash Days." (*Santa Barbara News-Press*, August 2, 2002)

Until the past decade, it was absolutely unthinkable for any Chumash tribe to contribute anything to any cause. It was not until the 1960s that the reservation even had running water. The poor plot of land has never had any obvious means of making money, and was basically isolated and ignored by the surrounding Santa Ynez Valley community. As put by Jeff Bradley, a long-term local in the area:

> Well when I was a student at UCSB in the early 1980s and living in Goleta, I had occasions to visit the Chumash reservation while involved in a Native Americans Studies course with Professor Inez Talamantez, who some of you may know. This is well before the first bingo hall, or any notion of a gambling facility. I don't need to tell you how poor the people who lived here then were. I distinctly recall one particular visit, a gathering, many years ago, on Barren Hill, just about this meeting hall, where Tiajuana Street is, where we now have many fine homes situated, and I remember just how little those families had. (*Public Comment Hearing,* Chumash Casino Bingo Hall, May 10, 2002)

During the past decade, however, the federally recognized Chumash tribe has dramatically altered its status of deprivation and hardship. Today, the Chumash Casino "has obliterated poverty, and the tribe is getting newfound respect" (*Santa Barbara News-Press,* December 28, 2001). These changed circumstances have enabled the recognized Chumash tribe to revitalize and promote its cultural heritage, and this self-confidence has seeped into the consciousness of other Chumash peoples.

So, despite the economic setbacks resulting from nonrecognition by the federal government, there is a revitalization of interest in Chumash culture, traditional customs, and local politics by all Chumash tribes as well as local non-Indians. No doubt the success of the casino has played a part in this resurgence of activities and identity politics. A cover story in the local Santa Barbara weekly newspaper, *The Independent,* stated:

> [T]here's no shortage of pride for any of the Chumash people, whose ancient baskets are considered among the best and most durable in the world; whose canoe-building and navigational skills were known seafarers from Seattle to San Diego, whose cosmological outlook produced the most vibrant of native legends and vivid of dances and songs; whose hunting and gathering expertise sustained a most bountiful menu in all seasons.
>
> With such a rich cultural heritage to pass along, the Chumash resurgence, while still relatively young, is expanding with such vigor and strength that these true Santa Barbara natives may one day find themselves whole again, as modern people with real roots in the South Coast soils. (*The Independent,* July 25, 2002)

THE SANTA YNEZ VALLEY

While sitting in the recently opened *Patrick's Side Street Café* in Los Olivos, in the heart of the Santa Ynez Valley, and sipping a wonderful bowl of "asparagus essence" soup, my husband and I reminisced about how different the small rural town is now compared to when I first visited it in 1995. Los Olivos, with a population of about 800 permanent residents, has been for the last 20 years a place of passing interest for the thousands of people visiting the wineries that surround the town's local district. However, in recent years Los Olivos has changed dramatically in tone. From a rather sleepy town offering sandwiches, newspapers, gasoline, and a few wine-tasting centers, it has turned into an upscale, busy lunch spot for a clientele interested in tablecloths, elegant wine glasses, and soufflé desserts. Fess Parker's restaurant epitomizes the changes with its wide veranda, overhanging baskets of bountiful flowers, fancy dinner settings, and expensive meals. On a sunny Sunday afternoon, the fleet of BMW, Mercedes, and Volvo cars lined up outside the restaurant speaks volumes about the socioeconomic class of people now attracted to the town's upscale services and the surrounding bed-and-breakfast lodgings, day spas, art galleries, antique boutiques, horse ranches, and vineyards where the average bottle of wine costs more than $20.

As we sat sipping soup, we chatted with the waitress about the changing nature of the town. She said she had lived in the area for some years and agreed that over time things had changed dramatically. Housing prices had shot up, and the rental market lacked opportunities. She mentioned that the restaurant in which she worked had changed ownership in quick succession due to the high leasing costs sustained by a strong market demand for more upscale establishments. I asked her if she thought that the Chumash Casino had had any impact on what was going on in Los Olivos or the Santa Ynez Valley more generally. She was not sure about the casino's impact, but she was certain about the different kinds of people who visited the casino versus those who visited Los Olivos and the wineries. In her opinion, they were entirely separate groups with very different leisure pursuits (though technically both the consumption of alcohol and the consumption of gambling can lead to addiction, and in that sense both can be classified as "drugs"). According to our waitress, the casino visitors were not interested in wines and expensive lunches, and visa versa. She said, "They catch two different buses," referring to the two free bus services to either the wineries or the casino from towns such as Santa Barbara and Lompoc.

About six miles southwest from Los Olivos lies the town of Solvang, which has made its name as a Danish village community featuring bakeries, restaurants, and a huge array of small boutiques selling anything with a supposedly European flair. With a population of over 5,000 residents, it is a bustling center of activity, particularly on the weekends, and ranks as one of the state's leading tourist destinations. The Solvang city council is in general very antagonistic to the casino expansion, fearful that the casino will attract the wrong sort of people and threaten Solvang's healthy tourist industry.

Approximately three miles east of Solvang is the smaller and quieter town of Santa Ynez. Founded in 1852, the town has a population of 4,000 residents and boasts historic western-style buildings, surrounding vineyards, and ranches. It also has clearly seen a great deal of housing development over the past few years. Many of these houses ring the hills surrounding the Chumash reservation, which is down in a lower valley adjacent to the town. In effect, the town's recent development has encroached upon the reservation, boxing it in.

On a sunny Sunday afternoon, the Chumash Casino, like the town of Los Olivos, is very busy. While driving through the reservation, I noticed that in contrast to the fancy atmosphere of Los Olivos and Solvang, the reservation facilities are modest and rather rambling, with a maze of what looks like temporary buildings, and old and new construction zones dotting the landscape (see Figure 4.4). Unlike Los Olivos, there are no green lawns or abundant flower boxes. The atmosphere is one of serious intent as cars turn off Highway 246 and enter the reservation along a road that is carefully policed by guards waving the cars toward the new five-level, 995-space parking lot. Even with this large new facility, I had trouble finding a parking spot (see Figure 4.5). Once I had parked, we joined all the people making their way briskly

Philip C. McCarty

Figure 4.4 Overview of construction at the Chumash Casino, 2002

Philip C. McCarty

Figure 4.5 The parking lot at the Chumash Casino, 2002

from the parking lot along a covered walkway toward the door of the casino floor where a friendly but firm security officer told my husband he could not enter with a camera.

The original 1994 Chumash casino was a tentlike structure. Today this has grown to three large gaming rooms that contain a bingo hall, a poker corner, and other more specialized areas. The structures are reminiscent of large bubble-style tents, and there is a feeling of temporariness. The casino employs 750 people, mostly non-Indian, who live in the local communities outside the reservation. The casino, the only Indian gaming casino between Los Angeles and San Francisco, serves about 3,500 visitors a day, which includes people in private cars as well as a large number who use the free bus shuttle from the cities of Lompoc (pop. 41,000), Santa Maria (pop. 80,000), and Santa Barbara (pop. 90,000). To give you an idea of the flow of people, the bus service from Lompoc and Santa Maria runs approximately every hour, and the last bus leaves the casino nightly at 1:00 A.M.

A large number of the casino clientele using the free buses are Latino. This in part reflects the enormous house prices in coastal Santa Barbara, which have forced many recent immigrants to move to Lompoc and Santa Maria where the costs of housing and general services are much less. These cities have flourished in recent years, and one of the attractions for residents without cars is the free transportation to the casino. For lower-income clients, the casino offers a day or night out at relatively low cost, along with the possibility of winning door prizes and perhaps a quarter slot machine jackpot. However, on a Sunday afternoon, the clientele can be summed up as "middle America," with Anglo visitors outnumbering those from obvious Latino or other minority backgrounds. One undergraduate student from the University of California, Santa Barbara, told me judgmentally that the casino clientele are all "trailer trash."

THE CHUMASH CASINO AND CURRENT PLANS FOR ITS EXPANSION

The plans to expand the current casino facilities have been the center of controversy for four years. Over that time, flare-ups have periodically errrupted between the local non-Indian Santa Ynez Valley communities and the Chumash tribe over a range of issues that are said to have an impact on the entire Valley. These issues have included the "inappropriate" appearance and aesthetics of the expansion plans; the increase to traffic on Highway 246 from which clientele enter the casino; higher demands on police, fire, and ambulance services to the casino; increased criminal activity in the area; and heightened air pollution and sewage problems due to the volume of customers visiting the Valley.

The original plans include a five-story, 72,000-square foot hotel with 120 rooms; a two-story, 155,000-square-foot casino with partial underground parking; and a 35,000-square-foot administration office building (see Figure 4.6). According to the architects of the hotel, the rooms will be luxurious, with French windows and spacious surroundings: The hotel "will provide the best accommodations in the entire Valley" (*Santa Barbara News-Press* August 6, 2002). In an attempt to alleviate local community concerns, the tribe has agreed to scale back the original plans. Currently the hotel will be reduced to four stories high, hold only 105 rooms, and sit alongside

APS ARCHITECTS, INC.

This drawing shows the planned Chumash Casino expansion with Highway 246 in the foreground.

Chumash to build hotel at casino

Complex would be higher than parking structure

By CHUCK SCHULTZ
NEWS-PRESS STAFF WRITER
e-mail: cschultz@newspress.com

Although Chumash tribal officials said in February there was no immediate plan to build a hotel as part of a casino expansion in Santa Ynez, plans released this week show a 106-room hotel atop a new 190,000-square-foot

casino.

The huge complex would be 16 feet higher than a five-level parking structure erected last year next to the existing casino. The plan to replace that casino with a bigger one is sparking renewed criticism from the community.

"We were aghast at the the size of the casino expansion to begin with," when

the initial plans were disclosed in December, said C.J. Jackson, co-chairman of the Santa Ynez Valley Concerned Citizens group. "Now the plan includes a new wrinkle that has got the people of this valley really upset," he added, referring to the proposed hotel. "It's just an enormous, dense development that is out of place with the rest of the valley."

The new facility, adjacent to

Please see **CASINO** *on* **A9**

Figure 4.6 Front page article on the planned casino expansion.

the casino rather than on top of it. Two of the three existing casino buildings will be demolished, as well as a number of existing administration offices.

In addition to the construction changes made in an effort to appease local community concerns, two other planned buildings are to be moved. These are the new tribal hall and the health clinic, which were to be built north of the casino on the other side of Highway 246 on 6.9 acres of land purchased by the tribe in the mid-1990s. In December 2001, American Indian skeletal remains were discovered beneath the site. After calling in the coroner's office for verification, the tribe decided against the project. As tribal chair Vincent Armenta commented, "We don't want to destroy our culture. We want to protect our culture" (*Santa Barbara News-Press* Jan. 18, 2002:1). Now the plans incorporate the building of a tribal hall and health clinic, each approximately 10,000 square feet, on the south side of the highway on the main parcel of reservation land. The tribal hall will house administrative offices, a conference room, an education department with desktop computers, and a new kitchen. The medical center will provide health care facilities for Native Americans as well as for the entire Valley. When it officially opened on December 12, 2002, Democratic state assemblywoman Hannah Beth-Jackson told the gathered audience of tribal leaders, local residents, and politicians, "It's a blessing and a gift to have these facilities. . . . We are all truly part of this community and I thank you for what you're doing for everyone in this community." Sarah Moses, a Chumash tribal member, stated more personally, "People now don't look at us like we're nobody—we're somebody" (*Santa Barbara News-Press,* Dec. 13, 2002).

Despite local opposition to the expanded casino and hotel, on July 15, 2002, bulldozers and tractors started cutting into ground on the Chumash reservation in preparation for the first stage of building. It is anticipated that construction will take more than a year to complete. Significantly, this project made history with its financing through $150 million bonds sold to mutual fund and insurance fund managers. As was noted in the local paper, "It is the first time in California that a bank has under-written a bond sale for an Indian casino project" (*Santa Barbara News-Press*, August 2, 2002).

LOCAL RESPONSES TO THE CHUMASH CASINO EXPANSION PLANS

Not all communities deal well with change. This is often the case in rural areas where the pace of city living is not felt so explicitly as in urban settings. For many residents living in rural areas, change and difference are deliberately avoided, and this avoid-ance is part of the reason many live in the countryside in the first place. Those opposed to change are often called NIMBYs, which stands for "Not in My Back Yard." So it could be argued that local response in the Santa Ynez Valley to a casino of any sort, run by Indians or otherwise, would be greeted with outrage and dismay. This was the opinion of Harvey A. Englander, a political consultant and senior vice-president of the MWW Group in Los Angeles. He has worked for both concerned local citizens and on behalf of Indian tribes, so he has a wealth of experience with both sides of the Indian gaming debate. According to Englander, with respect to the local non-Indian opposition to the Chumash Casino:

> If instead of the casino in that location there was a 24-hour Super Wal-Mart, these people would be opposing that as well. So it's not so much in my opinion that they're opposed to gaming, as much as they're opposed to anything that changes their immediate standard and way of life. . . . And of course they are dealing with guilt because, oh, they're picking on the poor Indians who have been oppressed for so long. So, there's a conflict there. For the most part, I see the tribes have been very positive participants in the community. But as I said, whether it's a community casino or a Wal-Mart, the people who live nearby do not want it intruding on their way of life. (interview, June 4, 2002)

The claim that local Santa Ynez Valley communities will react negatively to any change may be in part true. The communities are predominantly rural. The people are proud of the rolling hills and natural landscape dotted with neat farmsteads, expan-sive horse stables, and row upon row of beautifully manicured grapevines and wealthy estates. Still, the overall tone of the Valley has changed dramatically in recent years with a growing population, a boom in the building of strip malls and businesses as well as housing, and the expansion of small towns into bustling tourist centers with art galleries, spas, restaurants, and service businesses. Of course, the casino is on a bigger scale than any other project that has been built in the area, but its aesthetic "inappropriateness" is overrated; it is really no more out of place than the large strip malls, supermarkets, and huge parking lots now located throughout the region. In other words, there has been such dramatic change in the Valley in the past decade that change alone does not seem to explain the bitter opposition to the casino among the locals.

One explanation for local opposition is that the casino does not represent the right kind of change, but rather attracts the wrong sort of people, both as its clientele and its employees. Approximately 750 people are employed by the casino, and presum-ably this number will increase in the coming years as the casino expands. Many of these employees bus in from Lompoc or Santa Maria, along with the clientele on free bus shuttles. The employees tend to be loyal and defensive about their Indian employers. In the emotional words of one casino employee, Pat Lowry:

> I've worked in this Valley since 1973. I used to drive back and forth from Lompoc. . . . I now live in Guadalupe and I have a free bus ride to work. I've been here ever since the casino opened and have never had a better job, or made more money . . . there is no place at my age that I could work. . . . (breaks down crying; *Public Comment Hearing,* Chumash Casino, May 10, 2002)

Often referred to as "trailer trash," many of the casino's employees and clientele are from a lower socioeconomic class than Valley residents, and many come from different ethnic backgrounds, predominantly Latino. They do not drink wine at the vineyards, do not ride horses, and do not spend money at the expensive stores and local tourist attractions.

So one dimension of the opposition—one that is certainly not discussed openly— is that the casino represents an intrusion into the scenic and wealthy Santa Ynez Valley of a segment of the population that is not warmly embraced by Ronald Reagan's Republican cronies. This tension between a wealthy elite and a lower-income, largely ethnic population is not limited to conservative rural areas such as the Valley. Such tensions plague all southern California communities—rural, suburban, and urban. The disparity between the rich and the poor is extreme in this part of the United States, where the median price range for a home along the coast is now over $600,000, one of the highest in the nation. Yet, a large percentage of the state's economy is based on the work of poor, largely immigrant, Latino laborers who cannot afford to live in the very cities that employ them.

What makes local opposition to the Chumash Casino unique, and gives it a slightly different spin from the ongoing socioeconomic class battles present in almost all southern California towns, is that local resistance is often couched in implicit and explicit racist terms particular to Native Americans. The Chumash were tolerated in the Valley as long as they were subdued and played no role in local community relations and politics. Now that they are demanding a right to participate as a sovereign nation, many of the stereotypes discussed in Chapter 1 have surfaced in talk by non-Indians about the casino and its success. It is quite shocking that many of those opposing the casino are not even aware of their own cultural biases and prejudices that appear in their arguments against the Chumash and their successful gambling operations.

POSITIVE RESPONSES TO THE CHUMASH CASINO

Positive response to the casino are widespread, particularly among Santa Barbara County coastal communities that are not in close physical proximity to the Chumash reservation. There are also people living in the Santa Ynez Valley who clearly support it, though their voices may not be as loud and powerful as those of the people who oppose it. One group that has been constant in its encouragement is Santa Barbara's African American community. The president of the Santa Barbara branch of the National Association for the Advancement of Colored People (NAACP), Christine Simms, believes that the Chumash Casino is a great place, since the profits directly benefit the Native American community, unlike the profits of wealthy corporations that own casinos in other states such as Nevada. Moreover, the casino is well managed and controlled, safe, and serves no alcohol. According to Simms, Indian gaming is a way for Native Americans to provide economic stability where the government has not provided any other means of support or opportunities. The casino provides resources for education, homes, and jobs for Native Americans and non–Native Americans in the area. In Simms's opinion, since Native Americans view gaming as a business and entirely separate from their cultural practices, there is no negative impact on their cultural values (interview May 21, 2002).

Public comments on the casino expansion were heard on the evening of May 10, 2002, at a meeting held by the Chumash tribe in their large bingo hall. This meeting, intended to air and address local concerns, was required of the tribe under state law. Like most of the town meetings held in the past few years in the Valley, the meeting was well attended by those who are vocal in their opposition; only a few came to support the Chumash. The atmosphere at the meeting was clearly tense, with people huddled in corners prior to the start of the meeting, talking in hushed tones, and the tribal representatives remaining relatively quiet throughout. I am going to quote extensively from the speakers at this public meeting who were in favor of expansion because the manner in which these people expressed themselves and the arguments they used are worthy of close attention:

> My name is Richard Cochran. I've lived in Santa Barbara for almost 20 years, and tonight I thought I would come here to consider why you are all here, and ask you to consider that: what are you doing and what do you really want to accomplish? . . . [M]y great-grandmother was an Iroquois. Her tribe predates . . . the pyramids, the very act of writing, and in fact all that we're so proud to call history. This is not unlike the Chumash, whose guests we are here tonight, on sovereign land, in a sovereign nation. The Chumash have been forced off their own land, out of their mountains, and virtually out of this valley where they had lived peacefully for years. When I first came to Santa Barbara, someone stood with me at President Ronald Reagan's ranch at the top of the adjacent mountain, and pointed out important things in this valley. He told me there was a reservation there. . . . It has a look of despair and foreboding. Now our Chumash neighbors have bootstrapped themselves into something really remarkable. They have asserted not only their sovereignty as an independent nation, but created financial security for themselves, their children, and their children's children. They are working to ensure their futures as scores of others do and will work here. They're a damned generous lot too. No one twists anyone's arm to gamble. No one shot-gunned me off the highway to come here—I am not a gambler, I'm lousy at it. For those of you who came here tonight simply to quibble, you have that right. But again I ask you, what do you want to achieve? Maybe some here are NIMBY, and we all know what that means if you live in Santa Barbara. Or fewer of you are maybe a new species, the CAVE people, Citizens Against Virtually Everything. Or the new race, the BANANA people, Build Absolutely Nothing, Anytime New Anything. Unfortunate at least here too are bigots—it is an ugly word. I know bigots. As a small boy I watched a Klu Klux Klan march past my grandparents home, and no, I do not see a cross burning here, but I have heard with shame the same bigotry about what is going on here. Still others have genuine concerns. If those people of good humor could be filtered from such others, frankly I hear no unwillingness by the Chumash to do what is right for this land and their neighbors. After all, they've done a pretty damned good job. (Richard Cochran, *Public Comment Hearing,* Chumash Casino, May 10, 2002)

I see proud people, trying to make it so their children will prosper. Now I see a successful gaming operation, and a reservation that is giving back to the community. I am also one of the many local contractors that have been working at the res. I've worked on many million-dollar projects throughout California, and I can personally attest, the design, installation, inspection and quality control that is going on in this project is superior to any project that I've worked on—there's no shortcuts being made here. I support this project not because I have worked here, but because the tribe has a right to build here, it is their property. I also support the Concerned Citizens Group's rights not to support the project. But I do not support the right to make false or outright lies on what is going on down here to stir the community up. Once this project has completed landscapes, it will blend in like the high school gym, the Mission, or Albertsons [a supermarket]. I'm proud to be part of this community; just how I'm proud of what the res is doing for the people and the Valley. Thank you. (Mr. Williams, *Public Comment Hearing,* Chumash Casino, May 10, 2002)

Good evening, thank you for having us here tonight. Um, I'd like to address a recent article from County Supervisor Gail Marshall's office that ran in the *Santa Barbara News-Press.* The piece was a reply to an editorial that ran in the paper a few days earlier. First, the article states that, "All we want is for the Chumash tribe to keep the mitigation promises they made in exchange for a monopoly on the legalized casino gambling in Santa Barbara County." Monopoly? They were not given a monopoly. The Santa Ynez Chumash is the only tribe in Santa Barbara County. If there were more tribes in this county I'm sure they, too, would be given the right to operate casinos. Therefore the word *monopoly* is wrong. *Self-reliance* would have been more appropriate. Next, "The Casino operation has had and will have a profound effect on traffic, air quality, view shed, and other resources." That's correct! There will be an effect on traffic and the tribe had dealt with that by paying for the two stoplights as well as widening Highway 246. Keep in mind that these dollars are not coming out of our pocket. They are emanating from the pockets of those at the tribe. Okay, let's talk about air quality. Probably about a year ago the three townships here and the two cities got together to launch a campaign to promote this valley as a tourist destination. Since then, tourism here has actually increased. And with tourism comes cars and buses which, in turn, leads to poor air quality. So if you're worried about air quality I suggest we all speak to the folks over at Solvang City Council, and tell them to stop promoting Solvang because those tourist buses are botching up our lungs. I'm sure the store owners in the town would appreciate it as well as the gallery owners of Los Olivos [heavy sarcasm]. Next, view shed. What view shed? The tribe was given one of the scrappiest pieces of property here in this valley, and everybody knows it. There's no view shed— there never has been a view shed. To continue, some say that "Because previous generations repeatedly broke promises to Native American tribes, it's now okay for the Chumash to break the promises made to the community. We recognize and deplore the fact that the Chumash and other Native Americans were unjustly treated by all generations." Wrong! It's not just past generations, it's the current generation. How could all of us forget so quickly what this reservation looked like just a few years ago? The county roads here on the reservation were a disgrace. There was no money to upgrade the homes because many tribal members eked out a living bordering on the poverty level. Where were all the so-called "concerned citizens" then? For that matter, I don't recall seeing any of you concerned citizens when the tribe celebrated its 100th anniversary just a few months ago. You were invited. No, it's not just past generations—it's our generation and even those who follow in our footsteps. Just ask Chairman Armenta [Chumash tribal chairman], whose son was physically confronted at the high school. Why? Because he's a Native American. I'm embarrassed. Ms. Marshall's piece then continues with, "Two wrongs do not make a right, and the Chumash should make good on the pledges they have made to the community." What wrong have the Chumash done? Is trying to make a living wrong? Is taking care of your family wrong? Is trying to educate your children wrong? Is self-reliance wrong? I don't think so. As for making good on pledges to the community, they have. You've asked them to redo their structures—that's what they are doing. . . . [The planned structures will be] far more aesthetically pleasing than what it is we see here right now. Well, I guess to wrap up my comments I would just simply say that there has been more money that has emanated from the Chumash than any other group in this valley, and all of us, many of you, have come to them with your hands like this [shows hand palm up, as if asking for money]. I have seen very, very few of you, with hands like that [shows hand in position of shaking another hand]. But we thank you. (Lammy Johnston-Cuckler, *Public Comment Hearing,* Chumash Casino, May 10, 2002)

The Indian nation, a sovereign nation, on their lands, have tried to coexist with us for many, many years. I'm proud to say that my business is celebrating its 40th anniversary this May, and for many years I have come over and done commerce with the Indian tribe. I've seen the improvements in the housing. I've seen the improvements in the health care center. I've seen the improvements in the Indians themselves. They have looked to us, and found a way that they could get money to redo their houses, and build new houses, and become a part of this community. They've looked at their project, they've brought it tonight, laid it out and let you look at it, and we've made our comments. It's too big, it's too small, it's too high, it's too. . . . Let's all get together and get it resolved. Let's let them live their lives, as they have allowed us, their guests, to live our lives. (William Schuyler, *Public Comment Hearing,* Chumash Casino, May 10, 2002)

THE QUESTION OF COMPENSATION—"COUNTY WANTS SLICE OF INDIAN GAMBLING PIE"

Not surprisingly, at the heart of the controversy between the Chumash Indians and Santa Ynez locals is the question of money. The tribe is under no legal obligation to compensate communities surrounding its reservation for the impact of the casino on local services such as fire, police, sewage, and roads. Under Propositions 5 and 1A, as well as the subsequent compact signed between Governor Gray Davis and the Chumash tribe on May 16, 2000 (see the California Nations Indian Gaming Association's Web site at www.cniga.com), Indian tribes are only required to mitigate where feasible for local impacts. There is no mandatory assessment of these impacts or obligation to compensate for them. As stated in the report titled *Impact of the Casino Expansion on the Santa Ynez Valley,* issued by the Chumash on May 30, 2001:

As a result of federal and state laws and several significant Supreme Court cases the County has no regulatory authority over land use, environmental protection, intensity and density of development, design, landscaping or other normal onsite concerns. Likewise it has little or no authority to require the Tribe to mitigate offsite impacts of new development such as traffic, housing, parks development, public safety response times, and school facilities. Should the County disagree with the Tribe on impacts of development, its only appeal is to the Governor of California or special regulatory agencies. . . .

Despite the Chumash being under no official obligation, the tribe has made efforts to mitigate local concerns through charitable contributions, either as one-time capital infusions or contributions financed over time. Such mitigation involves a range of donations, such as $300,000 a year for five years, or a total of $1.5 million, to pay for an additional firefighter in the local fire department. There is also talk of paying for a fire truck. In addition, the tribe has agreed to put in two traffic lights on Highway 246 as well as widen the road at the entrance of the casino to help with traffic problems, though many locals see this as causing more harm than good and claim that the tribe has no right to mess with the road system. Often overlooked is the fact that CalTrans has an easement over the stretch of Highway 246 that runs adjacent to the reservation; this piece of road is technically Native American land. In response to local concerns about the aesthetics of the new buildings being built, the tribe has modified its construction plans, as mentioned earlier, in order to make the project appear more appropriate to the surrounding landscape. However, may locals think this is inadequate and that the new casino will be an "eyesore" and blight on what is constantly talked about as the Valley's "idyllic rural landscape." Such critics somehow forget that Indians themselves may have felt the same way about the Valley before the settlers came.

Apart from contributions relating directly to the casino expansion, the Chumash tribe also gives over $1 million annually to a range of public benefit organizations in the community, helps with the upkeep of high school sports fields, and provides funds for high school band uniforms. This is an extraordinarily large amount of money that is unmatched by any other local business concern in the Santa Ynez Valley. This fact is often ignored by local residents, or else they interpret the voluntary giving of money to nonprofit organizations as a purely political gesture made with insincere or manipulative intent. But the question is, when are monies donated to charities by any business organization given for purely philanthropic purposes? There is always an underlying self-interest on behalf of any capitalist enterprise contributing financial support to a charitable group, be it in the form of a personal tie and commitment to a local community, or a corporation's desire to promote its own image or popular appeal. To denigrate the Chumash Indians' contributions on this basis seems somewhat naïve and petty, particularly when the tribe can claim to be following the model of other successful Anglo-American capitalists. According to Gail Marshall, 3rd District county supervisor, and one of the most vocal political opponents to the casino:

> I guess in this whole thing, I just wish we could all be honest with each other. I just wish that we could all really try to work together. But that's not the tactic taken. They've [the Chumash] taken this sort of public relations firm attack, and that is to attack anyone who's against them, and favor those who don't speak out against them. And for that reason, you know, certain groups are granted monies for very beneficial things. . . . They've given a lot of money to non-profits, as long as you don't speak out against them. (taped interview May 13, 2002)

Although the tribe is not obligated under federal and state law to give directly to the surrounding local community to mitigate any casino impact, it is legally obligated under law to contribute to both the Revenue Sharing Trust Fund and the Special Distribution Trust Fund. The first of these, the Revenue Sharing Trust Fund, states that each tribe in California that does not hold a gaming compact, and so does not engage in casino activities, is to receive $1.1 million per year. This money comes from mandatory contributions made by tribes with casinos, and the intention of this fund is to ensure that Native American wealth is somewhat evenly distributed across all federally recognized tribes. The second fund, the Special Distribution Trust Fund, requires all tribes with casinos to contribute a percentage of their annual income to a fund to be distributed by the state for gambling related compensation. In section 5.2 of the required compact, tribes involved in Class III gaming must contribute to funds that will offset costs to governmental agencies regulating tribal government gaming, and generally contribute to local governments dealing with increased costs relating to fire, police, sewage, roads, and other related services. Some of this money is also distributed to help people with gambling addiction and to provide cheaper housing, recreation, youth and senior services, as well as child care.

Unfortunately, the legislature has been very guarded about how these funds will be distributed, which has caused anxiety among local governments eager to secure compensation for what they see as the burdens of a tribal casino on local resources. Statewide, the fund is estimated to be between $40 and $48 million. But according to Jennifer Klein, attorney assistant with the county counsel's office, "Because the question of distribution sits with the state Legislature, there is a possibility that all of the money will never come back to us. We're just nervous that the state might see this big pile of money as a way to fix the deficit" (*Santa Barbara News-Press,* August 14, 2002).

We should not forget, in the midst of this political confusion, that the distribution of compensatory funds back to local communities has been technically paid for, under state law, by tribes with casino operations. So if the money does not actually get distributed back to local governments and community groups by the legislature, this is not the fault of the Chumash, but rather of the democratically appointed California state government. No non-Indian casino operator in Las Vegas or Atlantic City has ever been forced to pay for providing services for gambling addictions or for health, recreational, or housing amenities. Tribes are being held to higher community standards than other entrepreneurs and capitalist enterprises, whether or not they are related to gambling. This reality directly contradicts popular attitudes that Native Americans do not pay taxes. According to my survey results, 40 percent of those interviewed believed Native Americans do not pay taxes, and 25 percent did not know (Darian-Smith 2002). But as argued by Ernie Stevens, tribal councilman of the Oneida Nation:

> The federal law requires tribal governments to use gaming revenues to fund tribal services such as education, law enforcement, tribal courts, economic development, and infrastructure improvement. Much like the revenues from state lotteries, tribal governments are also using gaming profits to fund social service programs, scholarships, health care clinics, new roads, new sewer and water systems, and adequate housing. In essence, gaming revenue serves as tax revenues for tribal governments. Like state and local governments, the revenues accruing to tribal governments are not taxed. State lotteries bring in $15.5 billion annually, more than five times as much as tribal gaming. Why is no one suggesting a federal tax on state lottery revenues? Governments should be treated equally. (Stevens 2000:173–174)

NEGATIVE RESPONSES TO THE CHUMASH CASINO

Although financial compensation and economic competition are at the heart of the bitter battles between the Chumash Indians and local Santa Ynez residents, many other arguments against the casino expansion have been raised. The charge against the Chumash Casino appears to be led by the Solvang city council, which represents primarily local business interests, as well as a group called the Concerned Citizens of Santa Ynez. In an interview with C. J. Jackson, president of the Concerned Citizens group, Jackson mentioned that the group formed in 1997 as a result of the Chumash buying land on the north side of Highway 246. This organization, which started with around 25 members who are the "worker bees" and do all the running around, receives direct contributions from around 250 people with a more hands-off relationship to the organization. C. J. Jackson is a businessman, with a bachelor's degree from Yale and a master's of business administration degree from Rutgers. He has lived in the Valley since 1985, though his family has run a business in the area for many years (interview May 3, 2002). Perhaps not coincidently, C. J. Jackson is the son of Palmer Jackson, who owns Alisal Ranch in Solvang. This is an exclusive guest ranch that offers 73 private cottages from $395 to $475 a person per night, as well as other amenities such as an on-site golf course, lake, spa, pool, petting zoo, and tennis courts.

It is doubtful that the luxury hotel being built by the Chumash tribe a few miles away from Alisal Ranch will compete directly with Alisal for customers. Nonetheless, the Chumash hotel and casino is a potential contender as a tourist attraction, and will certainly offer accommodations cheaper than those at places such as Alisal Ranch and other posh hotels in Solvang. As Harvey Englander, a political consultant, mentioned in an interview:

> Well, to me, there's no such animal as a citizens' group. . . . [A] citizens' group still needs funding, and while they may have feet they don't have dollars. And so there has to be an outside special interest, a financial interest, who will come up with the money to form a front organization, and funnel the money through there. (interview June 4, 2002)

Whether the Concerned Citizens of Santa Ynez truly represents a cross-section of local residents or only a small, but powerful, elite who owns the major tourist businesses and dominates local politics is an open question. Certainly one should examine the situation from a critical perspective and ask whose interests the group really represents. Likewise, it is important to think about and analyze carefully the main arguments against the casino expansion, while trying to unearth the underlying assumptions about Native Americans held by those opposing the Chumash construction plans. In doing this, it becomes clear that opposition to the casino uses some very predictable language and formulaic opinions reminiscent of arguments used against Native Americans more generally over the past 200 years.

Moreover, opposition to the Chumash casino expansion does not follow strict party politics. Historically, the Democratic Party has been more sympathetic and supportive of Native Americans and their concerns than the Republican Party. However, it is not helpful to assume this connection. For instance, Gail Marshall, Democrat and 3rd District County Supervisor, in the lead up to a recall vote in the local Santa Barbara County elections held on November 5, 2002, voiced strong opposition to the Chumash casino project. The issues involved were very complex, centering around resistance to development of the valley landscape. While it is inappropriate to go into the election details in this study, it is important to note that both Democrats and Republicans continue to fall back on stereotypes and commonly held assumptions about Native Americans that sustain discriminatory practices. As a prominent local activist in the Santa Barbara community explained to me excitedly on the phone, "The Indians have contributed $30,000 already to the recall effort [against Gail Marshall]. They're players in all of this you know. . . ." My response is to ask why, as a community, we continue to find it improbable that Native Americans can be significant political players. Moreover, why shouldn't they be? The Chumash are as vested in their self-interests as much as any other special interest group, and clearly are prepared to side with the political party that best serves their immediate concerns. Their apparent lack of loyalty to a mainstream political party is not surprising, given that Democrats and Republicans have shown little interest in Native American affairs until very recently.

One of the main claims that surfaces repeatedly by those opposing the casino is that the Chumash lied about their intentions to expand the facilities to include a hotel, restaurants, and other amenities. The opposition claims that by lying, the Chumash revealed that they do not want to work together with others in the community. This shifts the blame onto the Chumash for an unwillingness to be part of a larger community, and so glosses over the long-standing attitudes of the past 200 years whereby the wishes of the Chumash were openly denigrated and ignored by the surrounding white population. As C. J. Jackson, president of the Concerned Citizens group and one of the most outspoken opponents to the casino, conceded, "One of the elements that we in this community have been chastised for, and probably correctly, from the tribe and from the people, is that we didn't listen to you. Since Proposition 1A, I assure you we have" (*Public Comment* Hearing, Chumash Casino, May 10, 2002). Despite sporadic acknowledgments, such as C. J. Jackson's, that the Chumash have not been welcomed into the Santa Ynez community until very recently, the overwhelming rhetoric is that the Chumash reject open dialogue and refuse to work as a "team." These arguments about Chumash noncooperation and dishonesty revitalize many stereotypes of Indians that paint them as scheming and cunning people who operate through stealth and deception.

> They [Native Americans] could have said it's our perfect right, it's our land, we're going to do it, you know, and get the politicians behind it. They didn't. They went to the people because that was the easiest way to get it. To get the people of the state to be behind them. They knew that would influence every legislator in the state, and it did. And they made a promise, and they broke it, because they're not doing what they're supposed to be doing. (Gail Marshall, 3rd District county supervisor, taped interview May 13, 2002)

> [Y]ou were never honest with us. This is a project of deception. You started off with just a parking garage, this big. Well, you may have the dream, but you already have the footprint for this project. And now, all of a sudden, a hotel is suddenly possible? Where did that come from, some cloud? I doubt it. This was well-thought-out, prematurely, before any of us had a chance to see it. . . . (Larry Musgrove, *Public Comment Hearing,* Chumash Casino, May 10, 2002)

> This valley and community need to grow, cooperate and to develop together, and that means working together. The feeling that we in the community, and certainly in the Concerned Citizens, [have] is that we have a project that is, for all intents and purposes,

inflicted upon us, not shared with us, not participated [in] with us. . . . I ask you to please consider a little more respect-credit to your neighbors for their ability to be open and responsive to working together. (C. J. Jackson, *Public Comment Hearing,* Chumash Casino, May 10, 2002)

There has been a lot of press conferences on both sides, and there's been a lot of sins on both sides, but there hasn't been much two-way dialogue. I've advocated dialogue since the last public meeting in December of 2000. As a matter of fact, I advocated it with the members of the tribal council at the Tribal Hall before that last meeting. I'll continue to press for expressive dialogue between the tribe and members of the community. We don't bite. The people in this valley voted a strong majority for Proposition 1A. I have volunteers, I have a moderator, and I hope that you'll let me know when you're ready. (Richard Crutchfield, *Public Comment Hearing,* Chumash Casino, May 10, 2002)

A second argument used by many opposed to the casino is that the Chumash tribe, and by extension all Native Americans, are "lawless" and cannot abide by the rules of decent citizens. This attitude is related to the long-established Anglo term *Indian giver,* meaning "not-for-keeps" and backing out on one's promise. According to my survey, over 30 percent of those interviewed do not think Native Americans are governed by law, or are unsure if they are (Darian-Smith 2002). The fact that Indians are governed by their own sovereign laws, as well as the laws of state and federal agencies, does not prevent uninformed statements such as C. J. Jackson's: "You have the problem that tribes don't pay property taxes, don't pay state income taxes, don't pay federal taxes. . . ." (interview May 3, 2002). Another instance of ignorance was displayed by Cheryl Schmit, director of the Stand Up for California campaign against tribal gaming, who wrote, "The Indian Gaming Regulatory Act permits without impunity tribal government leadership to transgress laws that non-Indian citizens enacted to protect the environment, their quality of life and the character of their communities" (*Indian Gaming and Community Rights,* October 26, 2002). Such comments suggest that tribal governments are lawless. Moreover, they imply that while Indians themselves may not be criminals, they certainly attract criminal activity into the area. The insinuation, which harks back to the 19th-century colonial rhetoric discussed in Chapter 1, is that Native Americans still do not really belong in our civilized society, since they do not recognize the common rules that govern law-abiding Americans.

The claim that the casino will attract criminal activity is a spurious argument. As the political consultant Harvey A. Englander pointed out, the threat of potential crime is used as a political strategy to persuade people against casinos, but in fact, such crime is very rarely a problem:

Well, [it's] one of the things you play on, whether it's true or not. . . . But, for example, if I were running a campaign against a [reservation] casino, I might say that you couldn't prosecute local crimes being committed [on reservation land]. They [Indians] can stop our police from investigating or going onto their property. Whether it's true or not, who knows, but it raises doubt. And when you raise doubt in a political campaign, people tend to vote no. . . . The truth of the matter is that the casino operators themselves don't want crime. Because if crime is being committed, and obviously the media will pick up on this, why would anyone go to the casino if there was a higher likelihood of them being a victim of crime? So in reality I think the areas right there at the casino are quite safe. (interview June 4, 2002)

Despite there being no evidence that the Chumash Casino as it currently exists attracts any crime, or that the expansion of it would attract crime in the future, local opposition is fixed on this idea:

> I don't know what [gaming is] going to do for you as a nation, I don't know what it's going to do for us as a community. I don't know how it's going to benefit our businesses. All I know is that it's going to bring a lot of other illegal activity with it. (Nina Courtney, *Public Comment Hearing*, Chumash Casino, May 10, 2002)

> Scares me to death to think you'd have a 120-room hotel here with no law enforcement, no jurisdiction here. Gambling is one thing, but all the effects of the world could really run rampant here with a hotel and absolutely nothing to stop it. Yes, that's what really scares me with crime when we've got the element of overnight people, you know, we could have the best little whorehouse in Santa Ynez right here. . . . (David Proxin, *Public Comment Hearing*, Chumash Casino, May 10, 2002)

The third argument often used against the Chumash Casino is that the tribal government, and its chairman Vincente Armente, are not capable of running an efficient and well-managed casino. In short, Indians do not really belong in corporate America; they are still unsophisticated, irrational, primitive, lazy, and greedy, and they should be happy with what they have. These arguments, quite apart from insinuating that Native Americans cannot be effective businesspeople and so do not belong in mainstream society, run contrary to the ideologies of capitalism which uphold that making money is the ultimate goal. It is rather ironic (but not surprising) that Santa Ynez developers and entrepreneurs have used noncapitalist arguments against the casino expansion, especially when their opposition is driven by the desire to protect their own economic self-interests.

> If we were to build a valley we're living in together, we must agree that all growth at some point has a natural limit. Beyond this limit, more change only brings trouble and greed. Constant growth is not a sign that things are getting better. A compulsion to grow is a sign that what you have now is not working. In this spirit, I would ask you to please re-examine what you see as a need to change from your present design to a yet larger and more impacted facility. My question to you, is something wrong with what you have now? Isn't this all enough? And if you need to change this, would it not be better to keep the facility at its present scale and seek out quality, rather than quantity? (Jeff Bradley, *Public Comment Hearing*, Chumash Casino, May 10, 2002)

> Indians should be happy with what they have and stop trying to make more money; nobody should have a free lunch. (interview with couple from Ben and Jeff's Flooring, Santa Ynez, May 3, 2002)

> [T]hey want to borrow a hell of a lot of money to build [the casino]. We don't know from who, but we think it is a gaming consortium out of Minnesota. If their projections are right then that's okay, but if their projections are wrong and they have business problems, who's there to call the shots. . . ? (C. J. Jackson, interview May 3, 2002)

> [T]he other thing is that these are not real sophisticated people, and I want to say that as nicely as I can. And I want to say that, prior to my involvement as an activist in the community, I wasn't very sophisticated on community impacts, and what things meant, what the long-term action and reaction was, but I'm much more educated and I do understand. But they are not only uneducated to the actions and reactions to the actions, but they don't

want to be educated. You know, they've all got brand new trucks and lots of money; they don't have to be. They're thumbing their nose at everybody. (Gail Marshall, 3rd District county supervisor, taped interview May 13, 2002)

The fourth argument that surfaces again and again is that if Native Americans really loved the land and had a spiritual affinity with nature, as they supposedly do, then how could they possibly be advocating for a large building development on their own reservation? In other words, the Chumash tribe's desire to expand the casino somehow denies their very legitimacy and authenticity as Native Americans. This kind of straw-man argument, which conflates Indian business practices with their relationship to land, is unfair and underhanded, particularly given the huge building developments that have sprung up throughout the Santa Ynez Valley over the past decade.

> The Chumash and other Indian nations claim to be the keepers of nature. How did massive buildings, hotels, restaurants, fit with this respect for the earth and the beauties of the earth? (Lewis Torres, *Public Comment Hearing,* Chumash Casino, 10 May 10, 2002)

> I'm a third generation of Santa Barbara native, and I see just a colossal, big, huge building project right in the middle of this pristine, beautiful rural valley that we all came here to love. I do not understand how native people can see this as some way of making our valley better. (Larry Musgrove, *Public Comment Hearing,* Chumash Casino, May 10, 2002)

> Many tribal governments have failed to accept responsible stewardship of the environment. . . . (Cheryl Schmit, *Indian Gaming and Community Rights,* October 26, 2002)

The fifth line of reasoning, which is related to the fourth argument about the environment, argues that if Native Americans are involved in business practices and politics, they will lose their culture and what makes them, in fact, "Indian." This kind of reasoning implies that true Indians must be poor, and certainly not involved in modern financial practices, if they are to be considered "authentic." This argument harks back to a romanticized stereotype of Native Americans as being, in effect, remnants of a prehistoric age—spiritual, communal, untouched and unblemished by the corruption of modern society. It undermines their capacity to operate as modern people and, at the same time, denies their capacity to participate in contemporary regional and state politics.

> [T]hey have, you know, taken up a really beautiful legacy of basketry and tommel buildings, and really interesting lifestyles and sort of erased it with one fell swoop. I'm not sure how it's going to affect their generations to come, but I have a feeling it's going to be very negative. Because when you get $300,000 a year for sitting on the couch watching a Lakers game, not working, you model that lifestyle to the next generations. I'm not sure what it's going to be like. They'll have money but I wonder what else. (Gail Marshall, 3rd District county supervisor, taped interview May 13, 2002)

What such commentators do not realize is that the only way for tribes to protect and nurture their cultural heritage is to find economic independence. Many tribes involved in gaming are building cultural museums and buying back artifacts that were stolen from them in the past and that now reside in non-Indian museums.

The argument that making money harms Indian culture demonstrates an inability or unwillingness to disconnect cultural values from business activities. Moreover, the argument reveals a deep sense of paternalism toward Native Americans, implying that *we* know what is best for *them*. What if, for instance, an increase in the income of Chumash Indians could be causally linked to a decline in their basket weaving? This claim would be hard to prove, but even if it was true, who are we as non-Indians to say that this is a good or bad thing? That we find the baskets attractive and hope they will continue to be made in the future is largely irrelevant. If we were to be consistent and apply this line of reasoning to ourselves, we could claim that we should stop our own capitalist enterprises because they have ruined our American culture, as evidenced by the fact that few people bake apple pies or knit sweaters anymore.

CONCLUDING COMMENTS

Despite the landslide victories of Propositions 5 and 1A in support of Native American self-determination, the general enthusiasm for Native American entrepreneurship among ordinary Californians has waned since 1998. As tribes have become more prominent and more aggressive in their bids to establish casinos and other commercial ventures, there has been a backlash against them at the local level. The Chumash Band of Mission Indians in Santa Barbara County is a specific instance where vocal local community responses trying to prevent Indian development are in conflict both with state and federal law, and with the long-term intentions of the tribe to expand their casino operations and compete for the lucrative Santa Ynez Valley tourist trade.

Native Americans are the most highly regulated and controlled group of people in the United States; they are subject to federal laws, state laws, and their own internal governmental procedures. Community groups opposed to Indian gaming, such as Stand Up for California, make incorrect claims when they argue that Native Americans could "bring a casino, a housing tract, a power plant, a nuclear waste facility. Tribes can build with impunity, at their whim, disregarding statutes and ordinances that protect the environment and the quality of people's lives" (*Los Angeles Times*, January 21, 2001).

No tribe could ever build power plants, casinos, or nuclear waste facilities without enormous scrutiny and monitoring by federal and state agencies. Unfortunately, the Stand Up for California lobby group falls back on long-standing rhetoric, harking back to the 19th and 20th centuries, of Native Americans being, in some sense, lawless and unregulated. As we have seen from some of the comments by local people living in the Santa Ynez Valley, Proposition 5, which grants tribes the right to provide gaming otherwise considered illegal if practiced off California reservations, is being interpreted by some as a floodgate that will grant Native Americans unfettered rights to transgress all sorts of laws. The success of Proposition 5 and its practical implications are cited by some politicians to fuel a rising popular hysteria that ordinary American citizens have in some sense been cheated by Indian tricksters and hustlers who know how to work the system. In the words of Craig Marla, spokesperson for a new initiative against Indian gaming in California, "The idea just is to level the playing field and not allow unregulated, uncontrolled gaming throughout California" (*Santa Barbara News-Press*, January 20, 2002). This demand to "level the playing field" is persuasive capitalist rhetoric, but contains blatant irony, given the history of Native Americans and their treatment by federal and state agencies that repeatedly took advantage of their subjugated position and exploited their lands in the name of the law.

At this point, it is impossible to determine what impact this local backlash against Native Americans will have. But as tribal members move off isolated reservations and demand an increasing presence and place in mainstream corporate ventures and urban lifestyles, I anticipate that antigaming lobby groups will increase their media visibility and their supporting political constituency. In short, the new respect granted Native Americans in California through the landslide victory of Propositions 5 and 1A may be short-lived and transient. The general population's ideological shift toward granting Native Americans increased sovereignty may turn out to be a measure extended only to Indians who remain geographically peripheral and socially isolated.

SUGGESTED FURTHER READING

Arnold, Jeanne (ed) (2001) *The Origins of the Pacific Coast Chiefdom: The Chumash of the Channel Islands.* University of Utah Press.

Darian-Smith, Eve (2002) Savage Capitalists: Law and Politics Surrounding Indian Casino Operations in California. *Studies in Law, Politics and Society* Vol. 26:109–140.

Darian-Smith, Eve (forthcoming) *Challenges to State Law: Surveying Local Attitudes about Indian Gaming in Santa Barbara County, California.*

Miller, Bruce W. (1988) *Chumash: A Picture of Their World.* Los Osos, CA: Sand River Press.

Walker, Philip L. and John R. Johnson (1994) The Decline of the Chumash Indian Population. In Clark Spencer Larsen and George R. Miller (eds) *In the Wake of Contact: Biological Responses to Conquest.* New York: Wiley-Liss. Pp. 109–120.

5/Rich Indians,
New Capitalists

INTRODUCTION

In this chapter I explore the importance of Indian gaming as a source of economic independence for Native American peoples. Economic independence is significant as an entrée into formal party politics and, more profoundly, as a means of sustaining Native American cultural and social heritage. In the current historical moment, no other option equivalent to gaming is available to tribes. As stated in a report on Indian gaming presented to the National Gambling Impact Study Commission in 1998, new enterprises that did develop on reservation land have largely failed

> due to poor market access, inadequate government stability, insufficient control over tribal assets, BIA mismanagement, or lack of labor and management skills. The challenges facing tribal efforts to gain control of resources and profitably exploit market opportunities have been and continue to be formidable. (American Indian Gaming Policy 1998:26)

So while a number of people, both Indian and non-Indian, may think gaming is not the most appropriate source of revenue for this country's indigenous populations, there is in fact very little choice for what remains the poorest and most deprived ethnic community in the United States.

In the 1960s and early 1970s, the political climate in the United States was marked by concerns with civil liberties and the international and local implications of the Vietnam War. Although this era is largely associated with African Americans asserting a place in mainstream society, it was also the period in which Native Americans began to mobilize and call public attention to their economic, political, and social plight. As historian Peter Nabokov notes:

> [B]etween 1964 and 1974 a series of demonstrations, road blockades, land takeovers, and building occupations from coast to coast amounted to a firestorm of Indian outrage against wrongs past and present. Local dissatisfactions and generalized resentments against government and white society burst into the public eye. Indian defiance was led by two new interest blocs: off reservation and urban Indians on the one hand, and Indian students on the other. In 1960 more than thirty percent of America's Indians existed outside of any

reservation; ten years later they totaled nearly half the U.S. Indian population. Suffering much the same racial discrimination, police violence, and unemployment as other minorities, Indians in the cities began fighting back. Joining them were the postwar generation of articulate, college-educated Indian youth. (Nabokov 1991:356)

During this period, the American Indian Movement (AIM) was established and secured a measure of political and civil equality for native peoples, including the right to vote through the Voting Rights Act of 1965.[1] According to Jimmie Durham, a Native American activist:

> Our resistance became nationally visible in 1969–70 with the takeover of Alcatraz Island. The trend increased over the next two years with the seizure of the Mayflower replica at Plymouth, Massachusetts on Thanksgiving Day 1971 and the occupation of the Bureau of Indian Affairs headquarters in Washington, D.C. on the eve of the 1972 presidential election. After the massive resistance at the hamlet of Wounded Knee in 1973, I became a full-time activist in the American Indian Movement. I was continuously incredulous at the way the American public seemed to welcome our struggle, although I was never surprised at their ignorance of what it was we were struggling *for*. Completely passive, even complacent, people felt that the "Indian struggle" was one they knew. It was one they had sympathy with, *as if it were their own,* and they *knew* we did not threaten them. We would not ask for a seat anywhere. (Durham 1992:435; Durham's italics)

Alongside the legal concessions made to Native Americans in the 1960s and 1970s, the last two decades of the 20th century brought a gradual shift in popular attitudes toward Native Americans, promoting indigenous spirituality, purity, and environmentalism (see Chapter 1). However, both the 1960s and 1970s legal reforms, and the attitudinal changes of more recent years, have not been enough to ensure social, economic, and political equity for Native Americans in mainstream American society. As I have discussed throughout this book, this is because enduring stereotypes of Native Americans continue to mask our dominant culture's inability, and unwillingness, to change the structural legal and political policies that continue to place native peoples in positions of discrimination and inequality. Given our current policies, Native Americans have little choice but to embark, where possible, in casino operations as a viable opportunity to make money. Without economic independence, Native Americans are caught in a systemic cycle of oppression, poverty, and marginalization that has existed since the earliest colonial times. Without economic independence, Native Americans are not able to participate in mainstream party politics, and certainly not able to participate in capitalist enterprises. Casino operations offer, at this moment in history, the only reasonable opportunity for Native Americans to achieve any semblance of respect and equity in our dominant society.

Since the introduction of tribal gaming, the marginalization of Native Americans is gradually changing, resulting in trade-offs for both Indian and non-Indian popula-

---

[1]Native Americans born in the United States were granted citizenship under the Snyder Act of 1924. However, since the Constitution left it up to individual states to determine who had the right to vote, more than 40 years passed before all states allowed Native Americans to participate in the democratic system. Even when allowed to vote, Native Americans were often prevented from voting by literacy tests, poll taxes, fraud, and threats that kept many away from polling booths. With the passing of the Voting Rights Act in 1965, and subsequent legislation in 1970, 1975, and 1982, protections were installed that granted non-English speakers and others who were formally disenfranchised the power to freely exercise their right to vote.

tions that were both unforeseen and unanticipated. Following is a discussion of some of the unexpected impacts of Indian gaming, in terms of both popular mainstream opinions of Native Americans and how mainstream capitalism is being forced to adjust and accommodate Native American entrepreneurs.

CAPITALISM AND THE DECLINE OF THE WELFARE STATE

The idea of a welfare state that would provide safety nets for homeless, sick, uneducated, and socially outcast citizens was a hallmark of responsible democratic government that emerged in the late 19th century (Hirschman and Sen 1997). Today, however, the U.S. public dismisses the idea of a welfare state as an archaic ideal (Robbins 2001). The safety nets have been all but dismantled. In this respect, the United States leads the world in a return to simplistic laissez-faire capitalist ideologies, where the only logic for action and change is economic profit. The idea of providing a social system—whereby people of all denominations, ethnicities, genders, and classes can expect minimum standards of health care, education, housing, and job opportunities—is largely a thing of the past. And with this passing, we are losing a sense that by helping those less fortunate than ourselves, society as a whole benefits.

Unfortunately, today there is very little public desire to build a society in which all can thrive and coexist. Capitalist ideologies permeating the public arena support this lack of public desire. One of the most pervasive and revered ideologies is that of individualism. The myth of individualism holds that everyone is born equal, and hence has equal access to health, education, and job opportunities. According to this logic, anyone can economically and socially succeed as long as he or she works hard. The flip side of this rationale holds that if you are poor, you have apparently chosen not to make money, and your lower socioeconomic standing is entirely your own choice. Therefore, problems such as poverty and illiteracy are an individual's burden, and society need not take any responsibility for the socially disadvantaged. Of course, people vary in the extent to which they hold individuals responsible for their economic plight, with political "moderates" being more inclined to concede that structural factors make it impossible to completely level the playing field. However, despite this conflict of opinions, a prominent theme in American politics is the belief that the poor themselves are, in most cases, responsible for their social standing in society.

However, if you stop and think about it for only a minute, it is clear that people are not born equal, nor do they have the same access to jobs and other resources. Think of the black youth born in the impoverished ghettos of south-side Chicago and compare his life opportunities with those of the white youth born in Beverly Hills. The danger of the capitalist ideology that claims all are born equal and have equal chances to succeed is that, in reality, it enables those in better socioeconomic positions to forget or overlook the structural and systemic inequalities that exist within our legal, political, economic, and social world. It allows us, as a society, to believe that there is one legal system free of built-in discrimination and inequity, available to all equally. (See the discussion in Chapter 2.) It allows those of us who are lucky enough to attend a university and look forward to jobs that will pay us enough to buy a house and car, travel, support a family, and so on to believe that we somehow "deserve" it. This ideology also portrays the ever-increasing gap between this country's rich and poor as something that is beyond our control and somehow inevitable.

More specifically, the myth of individualism and the notion that the poor deserve their fate allow mainstream society to be reasonably comfortable with the fact that Native Americans remain the most impoverished ethnic community in the United States. Historically Native Americans have had the lowest socioeconomic status, and they still do, despite the success of some tribal gaming operations. The myth of individualism also allows us to overlook the extreme conditions Native Americans have to battle against such as the underfunded Indian Health Service, an agency under the umbrella of the U.S. Department of the Interior. But as Tim Giago, editor and publisher of the weekly *Lakota Journal* states, "In exchange for giving up millions of acres of land the government agreed to provide certain services to tribes in perpetuity. These treaty agreements included health care, education and the funds to operate a tribal government. . . . This is not a case of generosity or charity by the United States, but the continuation and the fulfillment of legal and binding treaties" (*Santa Barbara News-Press*, November 28, 2002). Despite long-standing legal obligations, Margo Kerrigan, director of the California Indian Health Service, states that the Indian health agency receives three times less than the Department of Veterans Affairs and two times less than the Medicare and MediCal programs. "Indians were forgotten," notes Kerrigan. "California tribes, unfortunately, have the lowest funding per patient of all tribal regions in the country" (*Santa Barbara News-Press*, August 16, 2002). As a result of limited health coverage, medical problems such as diabetes and AIDS are extremely high among Native American populations and are predicted to continue to rise.

The capitalist myth of individualism diminishes mainstream social responsibilities for Native Americans and makes excuses for their continuing poverty. Moreover, the image of a wealthy and financially independent Native American clashes with conventional images of native peoples. Enduring stereotypes present them not as individual members of society (as individualism would have it), but as people with an identity rooted in a collective "tribe." A Native American is known first as Apache, Blackfoot, Iroquois, or Chumash, and only secondarily as mother, teacher, lawyer, plumber, banker, or businessperson. When a non-native meets someone known to be Native American, the standard question is not the usual "what do you do?" but "what tribe do you belong to?" These often unconscious distinctions white society makes with regard to Native Americans sustain the divide between "us" and "them." They make it difficult for a middle-class Anglo-American to imagine, let alone endorse, the idea of a Native American school superintendent, a Native American doctor, a Native American art dealer, a Native American real estate agent, or a Native American millionaire living on the upper west side of New York.

RICH INDIANS ARE NOT REAL INDIANS

Enduring stereotypes prevent mainstream society from imagining Native Americans in positions of power, authority, and social prestige. It is not surprising, then, that our dominant society also finds it difficult to imagine and support what some white Americans label "rich Indians." A rich Indian is considered somehow inauthentic and not "real"; such an image unsettles popular preconceptions of how Native Americans "are supposed to be." Anthropologist Katherine Spilde, a member of the National Gambling Impact Study Commission, has pointed out that the prevalent image of

Indians in this era of gaming on reservations is that of the "rich Indian." According to Spilde:

> This image assumes that all Native Americans are benefiting financially from Indian gaming, overlooking the fact that only one quarter of the tribes offer gambling and many tribal casinos are only marginally successful from a revenue standpoint. Of course, images are not meant to capture the facts. The purpose of the Rich Indian image is to undermine tribal sovereignty. Rich Indian rhetoric provides a language of racism in two contradictory ways. First, by insisting that gaming tribes no longer need sovereign rights (including hunting and fishing rights) to be self-sufficient. This argument relies on the notion of surplus (as defined by non-Indians) and shows up in legislation in the form of "means testing" which requires tribes to prove that they still deserve their sovereignty. Second, the Rich Indian portrayal argues that gaming tribes are less "authentically" Indian, diminishing their claims to any political independence implied by sovereign rights. The authenticity argument implied by the Rich Indian image rests on notions of class: Since "real" Indians are not wealthy, being "rich" means that some Native Americans are not sufficiently different from "other" Americans to deserve sovereign rights. (Spilde 1999)

The use of the "rich Indian" imagery was dramatically illustrated in the Republican-based political campaigns in late 1998 against Proposition 5. In the final weeks before voting day on November 3, it became increasingly clear that the lobby group against Proposition 5 was losing ground. In a panic, the opposition bombarded the population of California with a series of television and radio advertisements that represented Proposition 5 as a serious threat to a homogenous (white) American culture and established legal order. These advertisements deliberately played upon the capacity of Proposition 5 to redefine what it means to be a Native American and the extent to which it disrupts a reassuring colonial imagery of Indians as part of "nature," poor, suppressed, and spatially isolated on distant reservations. The ads stated in an alarmist way that Proposition 5 would result in unlimited, unregulated, and untaxed gaming; would increase crime; and would benefit only a few wealthy Indians, doing nothing for the poor. According to Tom Gorman, a reporter from the *Los Angeles Times:*

> The 30-second commercial opens with photographs of seemingly destitute Indians, followed by views of opulent houses on the San Manuel Indian reservation near San Bernardino, home to one of the state's largest Indian casinos. . . . San Manuel's vice chairman, Ken Ramirez, responding to the ad, said that tribal members are "hard-working responsible business owners" who have shared their casino revenue with the community. "This ad somehow depicts our lives as selfish and uncaring," he said. "We are far from that. The message of the Nevada casinos' deceptive ad campaign seems to be: the only good Indian is a poor Indian." (*Los Angeles Times,* October 27, 1998)

As mentioned in previous chapters, not all tribes run casinos, and of those that do, many are economically unsuccessful because of their geographical isolation from a sustainable clientele. Only a few of the 550 federally recognized Native American communities in the United States receive substantial incomes from gaming practices. These tribes, and in particular their new material wealth, stand out in the public imagination precisely because they disrupt the long-standing historical myths of indigenous people being completely different from the dominant Anglo-American population.

The image of rich Indians, along with the "lack of difference" between dominant and minority communities, raises all sorts of questions about the relative authenticity and legal legitimacy of Native Americans involved in casino operations. For instance, the Pequot Nation and their casino was the subject of a *60 Minutes* television program that aired on CBS on January 1, 2000. This program presented the Pequot tribe as inauthentic because they do not, apparently, look like "real" Indians. For this reason they were also presented as fraudulent for misrepresenting their status in seeking tribal recognition. The program quoted from Jeff Benedict's book entitled *Without Reservation,* in which Benedict argues that the tribe and its lawyers "pulled a fast one on the federal government, and that if Congress had been paying any attention at all back in 1983, when it gave the Pequots tribal status, it would have discovered that the tribe didn't meet the minimum requirements" (from *60 Minutes,* January 1, 2000, titled "Wampum Wonderland: Legitimacy of Casinos Run by Indians").

Related to the question of whether wealthy Native Americans can be "real" Indians is the argument that Indian gaming jeopardizes Native American cultures. When I discuss Indian gaming with my undergraduates, the most common and passionate response by students is that gaming on reservations will destroy Native American heritage. For many students there is a profound sense of betrayal or loss associated with the image of wealthy Native Americans, and outrage that as a society we are "allowing" native peoples to destroy what somehow belongs to "us." This outrage makes sense only if non-Indian populations believe (as they did in colonial times) that they own and control Native American cultures and histories, and are the most qualified arbitrators both of what these cultures are and how they should best be preserved.

Furthermore, public concern for preserving indigenous cultures appears shallow and hypocritical given the other ventures our society allows on reservation land (see Churchill 1999; Fixico 1998). These include the dumping of toxic waste, mining slurry, and household waste on reservations, as well as the draining of local water supplies that feed reservation lands such as Southern California Edison's Mohave Generating Station near Laughlin, Nevada. Bradley Angel, in a document prepared for the international organization Greenpeace, writes:

> Hoping to take advantage of the devastating chronic unemployment, pervasive poverty and sovereign status of Indian Nations the waste disposal industry and the U.S. government have embarked on an all-out effort to site incinerators, landfills, nuclear waste storage facilities and similar polluting industries on Tribal land. . . . Instead of conquistadors armed with weapons of destruction and war, the new assault is disguised as "economic development" promoted by entrepreneurs pushing poisonous technologies. The modern-day invaders from the waste disposal industry promise huge amounts of money, make vague promises about jobs, and make exaggerated and often false claims about the alleged safety of their dangerous proposals. (Angel 1991:1)

One of the most horrifying "new assaults" is the dumping of toxic waste around the Skull Valley Goshute Reservation, which lies about 80 miles northwest of Salt Lake City, Utah. Utah allows no gaming, be it on tribal reservations or not. The Goshute tribe currently has approximately 500 members, of whom 124 live on the reservation. Forty miles away from the reservation in one direction is Tooele Depot, a military site that houses 40 percent of the nation's nerve gas as well as other hazardous gases. Fourteen miles away from the reservation in another direction is the Dugway Proving Grounds, an experimental center that works with viruses such as the plague and tuberculosis. In a powerful essay, Randel Hanson writes:

> [N]early surrounding the Skull Valley reservation completely are lands made toxic by the U.S. military and various corporations in forms that will likely persist long into the future. This late-industrial colonization of the Skull Valley Goshutes represents a form of environmental racism that is little reported and less addressed, and the environmental, legal, and health dimensions of this toxificiation are yet to be revealed. As Leon Bear [tribal chairman] observes: "From all directions, north, south, east, and west, we're surrounded by the waste from Tooele County, the state of Utah, and U.S. society. Over 30 percent of the tribe is children, so yes, we're very concerned about the effects of all this." With such a density of toxins, combined with the relative remoteness of the reservation, attracting any form of economic development has been very difficult for the Goshutes. And this lack of economic activity on the reservation, combined with the attendant health hazards, in turn makes it very difficult for people to stay on the reservation. (Hanson 2001:28)

Currently the Goshute tribe is bitterly divided on whether to contract with Private Fuel Storage to build a privatized nuclear waste storage facility on reservation land to house 40,000 tons of spent fuel rods from out-of-state nuclear power plants (*New York Times* October 20, 2002:16). For those who support the facility, such as Leon Bear, the venture represents an opportunity to generate substantial revenue within the "very difficult and compromised set of circumstances that colonization has bequeathed upon the Goshutes" (Hanson 2001:26). And because Utah state politicians and surrounding reservation residents oppose the plan, it also represents an opportunity to assert the political and legal sovereignty of Indian lands. However, there are many Goshutes who object on the grounds that their reservation should not be permanently tainted as a storage facility for "material which advanced industrial society cannot come to terms" (Hanson 2001:26). These objections are made despite the bleak economic outlook for tribal members, and the potentially slow cultural annihilation of the Goshute people, if the tribe does not agree to nuclear storage on reservation land.

The case of the Skull Valley Goshute reservation is one of many such instances where reservations and surrounding lands are used as dumping grounds for nuclear waste, toxic materials, mining slurry, and household waste. Other tribes are having their sacred land sites desecrated by companies mining adjoining reservation water sources for geothermal plants, as demonstrated by the current legal battle over Medicine Lake in northern California between the Calpine Corporation and a coalition of the Pit River tribe and environmental groups. In November 2002, the Bush administration overturned an earlier 2000 decision made under Clinton, and gave permission to Calpine Corporation to develop a 48-megawatt geothermal plant. This was despite earlier findings that a power plant close to the lake could harm the tribe's cultural values and the surrounding scenic landscape. Vernon Johnson, a member of the Pit River tribe, was "disappointed that tribal concerns were brushed aside." But he was hardly surprised. "They've been doing that all along through history" said Johnson. "This whole system is corrupt" (*Los Angeles Times*, November 27, 2002.).

A particularly telling example of the shifting fate of Native Americans in the fight to preserve their sacred sites, health, culture, and dignity is represented by the Pala Band of Mission Indians in San Diego. In the early 1990s, the Pala tribe fought hard to prevent the establishment of the Gregory Canyon landfill near their reservation, arguing that it would be one mile from their sacred sites. Their pleas to surrounding San Diego residents not to support the landfill went largely unheard; 68 percent of the county voters approved the plan in 1994. However, with the passing of Proposition 5 in 1998, the Pala tribe decided to build a casino. The casino plan attracted powerful political lobbyists and backing from a Las Vegas company, and their collective clout stalled the landfill project. The temporary preventing of the landfill project, however, did not happen because people felt strongly about preserving sacred sites or questioned the fairness of using adjoining reservation land for dumping non-Indian garbage. Rather, these business interests were keen to keep the site around the reservation clean and attractive so as not to dissuade potential casino clients. What becomes clear is that accompanying the tribe's changing economic fortunes is a "newfound ability to assert long-held claims that their lands are sovereign." According to Pala tribal secretary Stan McGarr, "We are a sovereign people. But one of the things we've learned is that if you really want to be sovereign, you better have some money. People didn't used to care about us. But all of a sudden, we've got something to back that sovereignty" (*Los Angeles Times*, August 31, 2000).

ARE RICH INDIANS GOOD CAPITALISTS? DOING BUSINESS ON AND OFF RESERVATIONS

Many non-Indian Americans are concerned that Native Americans involved in capitalist enterprises will no longer conform to their conceptions of Native Americans being poor, removed from mainstream society, and uninvolved in formal political processes. As mentioned in Chapter 4, opposition to the Chumash Casino expansion project has charged that Native Americans are not capable of "handling" business transactions and participating fully in corporate America. In other words, Native Americans are often considered by mainstream society as not sophisticated or savvy enough to become successful business operators. Clearly, with the rise of lucrative tribal gaming operations, this assumption is not only patronizing and arrogant, but simply unfounded.

Despite mainstream preconceptions, tribes involved in gaming on their reservations are making a substantial impact on surrounding counties and adjacent businesses. Not only are they proving to be savvy business partners, but they also are forcing companies involved in gaming, such as those that supply slot machines or help establish casino security systems, to work on tribal terms and according to native practices. For instance, the Viejas Casino and Turf Club employs nearly 2,000 people (the majority are not Native American Indian), buys most of its goods and services from local non-Indian vendors, and plans to double its annual $500,000 donation to local charities and civic groups. Perhaps most significantly, the Viejas and other tribes are forcing outside companies interested in tapping into California's lucrative casino industry to reevaluate their selling strategies. Said Michael Lombardi, an attorney and a former manager of Indian casinos, "If you were going to do business in Mexico or Peru or China, you'd spend time studying those people and their culture, wouldn't you? . . . So when you develop your marketing strategies and your sales strategies . . . remember you're dealing with nations, you're not dealing with Indian casinos. . . . It's . . . about a new way of doing business with tribes" (DeArmond n.d.). This sentiment was endorsed by Norman DesRosiers, a tribal gaming commissioner for the Viejas tribe, who reminded gaming-industry officials that Indian gaming is not just another business: "You're not dealing with 60 casinos in California. You're dealing with 60 governments" (*The Press Enterprise,* March 21, 2000).

The idea that non-Indian companies must deal with the particularities of specific tribes was a hard lesson to learn for two firms that partnered with the Cabazon Band of Mission Indians to establish recycling plants on their reservation near Palm Springs, California. The companies and the tribe had financial disputes, and the companies filed formal complaints objecting to the arbitration of their contractual negotiations by the Cabazon tribal court. According to the tribe's director of legal affairs, Patrick Schoonover, "when businesses partner with Indian tribes, they are signing contracts with sovereign government entities with unique legal systems that differ from conventional civil courts where business disputes are usually resolved." Noted Schoonover, "Regardless of whether a particular party is unhappy with the. . . end result, that's the system we have" (*Los Angeles Times,* May 15, 2000). Outside California, it is very common for tribes to establish civil and criminal court systems that decide on legal issues within their reservation jurisdictions. In California, most tribes have not yet established their own courts, and so many non-Indian companies are caught unaware that potential disputes over contractual terms may be decided by a tribe itself. For this reason, the Bureau of Indian Affairs offers little advice to companies wishing to establish business relations with tribes. "Each side has its attorneys, and that's what they are paid for, to look out for those kinds of issues [involving business disputes]," said Ray Brown in the Bureau's Office of Economic Development in Washington, DC. "Our best advice is for [non-Indian businesspeople] to get attorneys who are familiar with these kinds of deals" (*Los Angeles Times,* May 15, 2000).

Despite the fact that some non-Indian companies are learning difficult financial and legal lessons when it comes to working with tribal governments, many have established very successful business arrangements and dealings with various tribes. These non-Indian companies are increasingly aware that contracts are signed between corporations and tribal governments, and often liabilities are determined within a tribe's own legal structures. Each agreement, be it between the state of California and a tribe, or between a gaming manufacturer and a tribe, has to be negotiated and modified to the specific requirements of the sovereign Indian community and its internal system of "customary laws."[2] Interestingly, Waltona Manion and Michael Lombardi, legal consultants to tribes with gaming operations, caution white business entrepreneurs looking to work with Native Americans that they must adopt a democratic perspective precisely because corporate America is not democratic:

[2]Tribal customary laws are also intertwined with modern state law, despite appearances to the contrary. Since the time of conquest, indigenous peoples have not lived in isolated pristine environments with legal "customs" entirely distinct from state legal codes. As noted by Sierra, "customary law—as the product of processes of domination, colonization, and resistance—is embedded in the dynamics of state law and the global society" (Sierra 1995:229).

In Nevada or Atlantic City, the management culture is highly competitive and a tough hide is a requirement to survive. But a tough, autocratic style won't serve you well in Indian country because ultimately you are not in charge. In fact, the very employees you supervise are, in effect, your bosses because they elect the council who hired you. Power flows from the tribal members to elected officials and it is the elected leadership who give you the authority to manage. But that authority is not a mandate for totalitarian government. Rather, it is a designation of trust that you manage with a fair and equitable approach. As De Toqueville noted when he wrote about the early days of American government, democracy can be inefficient. However that is precisely the environment in which you are working—a highly democratic process in which all levels of the organization have the ability to influence and direct the operation of the casino. Ultimately if you are uncomfortable with or can't respect this structure, you possibly should consider another work place. (Manion and Lombardi n.d.)

The success of tribal gaming has opened opportunities for Indians to participate for the first time in corporate America, and at the same time is forcing some American business and legal practices to become culture- and place-specific, grounded in the nuances of localized tribal jurisdictions. In conjunction with the new business practices and legal arrangements that are emerging between companies and tribes, a slight shift may be seen in the dominant capitalist ideologies that support early 21st century U.S. corporatism. The myth of individualism, for example, does not hold when dealing with tribal governments. Nor does the myth of one legal system, applicable to all United States citizens, hold in the face of tribal entrepreneurialism. As non-Indian companies are discovering, sometimes to their disadvantage, they must take into account multiple levels of legal jurisdiction—tribal, state, and federal.

Perhaps most interestingly, many tribal governments involved in lucrative casino activities challenge the idea of economic profits as the overriding rationale for all activities. This rationale has been the driving force in the decline of the welfare state and our loss of a sense of collective responsibility for society's less fortunate. In contrast to many other American businesses, tribes involved in gaming generally give substantial percentages of their profits on a voluntary basis to local non-Indian charities and community groups. In addition, California state law requires tribes with casinos to give a substantial percentage of their profits to tribes without gaming under the Revenue Sharing Trust Fund and the Special Distribution Trust Fund. This mandatory "sharing of the wealth" is a requirement not imposed on anyone else in the United States—no one forces Donald Trump to share his profits with disadvantaged minority groups.

The point is that there are emerging alternative models, if only on the margins of mainstream capitalism, of how to conduct business and distribute business earnings. Indian capitalism is forcing non-Indian companies that do business with tribes to recognize a variety of localized cultural and legal practices specific to a particular Native American community. Indian capitalism, by highlighting the complex differences between specific tribes across regions and states, is challenging the dominant image of one homogenous and encompassing group of people called "Native Americans." By promoting community service, charitable contributions, and the value of sharing the wealth among those less fortunate so that society as a whole may benefit, Indian capitalism is also challenging the dominant logic in which economic gain is the only result that matters.

WHERE IS "INDIAN COUNTRY"?
NATIVE AMERICANS IN MAINSTREAM POLITICS

The Democratic Party state convention, held in Los Angeles in August 2000 at the enormous downtown Westin Bonaventure Hotel, buzzed with activity thousands of people scurried around, bedecked in red-white-and-blue stickers and buttons and clutching brochures, bags, flags, and other political paraphernalia. People looked around excitedly, waving to friends, shaking hands with new acquaintances, and glancing anxiously at schedules and programs to determine where they should go in the labyrinth of conference and meeting rooms.

I attended the convention to talk with people from the Native American caucus of the California Democratic Party. The Native American caucus is the newest addition to the state party's 21 caucuses, and the only caucus of its type in the country. Talking to Raven Lopez-Workman, one of the driving forces behind the Native American caucus and its founding chair, I began to sense the significance of the caucus and all that it represents and symbolizes for some Native American communities. Lopez-Workman, a woman who claims to be a "native, native Californian" of mixed heritage, helped organize the youth vote for J. F. Kennedy in the 1960s. Since that time, she has been heavily involved with Native American issues. According to her, "no injustice is as great historically, or even today, as that against Native American communities." With Lopez-Workman's Native American background, activist history, and clear concern with social justice and issues of equality, the fight in California for tribal gaming in the 1990s provided a natural arena for her considerable energy. As she explained to me, at that time there was no organized political movement among California tribes in the fight against then Governor Pete Wilson and his Las Vegas casino backers who opposed Proposition 5.

The Native American caucus grew out of the political momentum generated by the landslide victory of Proposition 5 in November 1998. As discussed in Chapter 3, Proposition 5 granted California tribes the right to install Las Vegas–style gaming on their reservations. Thirty days after Proposition 5 was voted in by a 63 percent majority, Raven Lopez-Workman laid the groundwork for the Native American caucus, establishing by-laws, organizing tribal involvement, and seeking a variety of non-Indian forms of support. In her words, "there is something about pain and suffering that gives you drive." At the state convention in February 1999, Democratic Party leaders advised her to wait in her bid to seek party endorsement of the caucus; however, she persevered, and the Native American caucus received formal recognition that year.

In the year 2000, the California Native American caucus had 119 members, 20 of whom were tribal members. When I asked Lopez-Workman why there were not more Native Americans involved, she responded that "many Native Americans are fearful or do not understand the structure and venue for political reform." Despite the relatively few active Native American members, the caucus stands as a fitting symbol of the newfound political clout some Native American groups are forging in the wake of their economic independence, granted primarily by casino profits. The caucus has attracted considerable attention from other state Democratic parties, such as those in Arizona and Montana, that want to establish similar political forums and caucuses centered on Native American issues.

In the large auditorium at the Westin Bonaventure Hotel where the Native American caucus held its business meeting at the 2000 state Democratic Party convention, a constant stream of candidates arrived with their entourages of supporters, passionately declaring why people should vote for them. Candidates seeking statewide endorsement clearly thought it desirable to convince the Native American caucus that they would best represent its interests. Given that the caucus was so new, the candidates' recognition of it and their wooing the support of the Native American caucus represented a political triumph for Raven Lopez-Workmanand others like her who fought so hard to formalize, politicize, and gain acknowledgment and recognition of Native American concerns within the Democratic Party. (There has been no such successful movement within the Republican Party.)

The recent involvement of Native Americans in the official political process of the United States, and the increasing interest in Native American issues by non-Indians as well, could be optimistically interpreted as an indicator of shifting attitudes toward the country's indigenous communities and a willingness to listen to and support them. However, I favor a more cynical, but perhaps more realistic, interpretation. With some tribes engaging in lucrative gaming operations and contributing significant amounts of money to Democratic (and Republican) political campaigns, more and more candidates realize that they cannot, quite literally, afford to ignore Native American issues. In short, with the profits from gaming on reservations, Native Americans hold, for the first time, some political presence precisely because they now have sufficient economic clout to force the mainstream political process to take them seriously. Lopez-Workman succinctly summed up this situation when she said, rather bitterly, "many people think of Indians as a political checkbook."

Whether one takes an optimistic or more cynical view about shifting attitudes toward Native American peoples, the point is that no longer are indigenous communities entirely relegated to faraway reservations, out of sight and out of mind, and out of public view. The 19th- and 20th-century colonial attempts to keep native peoples separated from mainstream society on reservation land, in so-called Indian country, are clearly failing. There are great advances to be made before Native Americans are treated equally by other American citizens. However, with the introduction of lucrative Indian gaming operations, small steps are being taken, and there is an emerging hope that one day we will move beyond reservation mentality and the entire United States will be considered "Indian country."

SUGGESTED FURTHER READING

Churchill, Ward (1999) A Breach of Trust: The Radioactive Colonization of Native North America. *American Indian Culture and Research Journal* Vol. 23(4):23–69.

Fixico, L. Donald (1998) *The Invasion of Indian Country in the Twentieth Century: American Capitalism and Tribal Natural Resources.* Niwot, CO: University Press of Colorado.

Hanson, Randel D. (2001) An Experiment in (Toxic) Indian Capitalism?: The Skull Valley Goshutes, New Capitalism, and Nuclear Waste. In Susan Gooding and Eve Darian-Smith (eds) Putting Law in Its Place in Native North America; Symposium. *Political and Legal Anthropology Review (PoLAR)* Vol. 24(2):25–38.

Hirschman, Albert O. and Amartya Sen (1997) *The Passions and the Interest.* Princeton: Princeton University Press.

Robbins, Richard H. (2001) (2nd ed) *Global Problems and the Culture of Capitalism.* Boston: Allyn & Bacon.

6/Local Implications, Global Connections

In this case study I have begun to explore the political, legal, social, and economic controversies surrounding gambling on Native American land. There are many important issues facing Native Americans today, including extreme poverty; acute unemployment; high rates of disease and mortality; encroachments on traditional water, hunting, fishing, and whaling rights; and the use of reservations as toxic dumps for nuclear waste. All of these pressing issues are productive sites for the examination of relations between Indian and non-Indian populations in this country. I chose to focus on the issue of Indian gaming precisely because the financial success that gaming brings fundamentally challenges dominant cultural attitudes about what it means to be Native American in the 21st century. Indian gaming forces us to reconcile persistent stereotypes of Native Americans with a new reality: that of natives as successful entrepreneurs and tribes as influential corporations. Indian gaming is an ideal site through which to explore and discuss shifting attitudes and emerging popular opinions about much larger questions: Who is Native American? What is "authentic" Indian culture? Who has the right to legally determine whether or not Native Americans can participate in modern capitalism?

This case study demonstrates the huge shift in future prospects that has occurred for the indigenous communities of the United States since the introduction of Indian gaming in the late 1970s and early 1980s. This shift has occurred even though only a small number of Native Americans are directly involved in gaming operations, and even though the tribes who have directly profited from casino activities remain relatively few in comparison to the entire Native American population across the country. However, these few tribes have succeeded, directly and indirectly, in forcing American society to take Native American entrepreneurs seriously as potential business partners, and as potential equals in mainstream politics, economics, and public media. As Victor Rocha, a Pechanga tribe member, notes, "You get the justice you can afford. We can finally afford justice" (*Los Angeles Times,* February 10, 2003).

The enormous impact made over the past few decades by tribes with casinos is evident in the many states that allow Indian gaming. For instance, in Oregon, all but one of the state's tribes have casinos, and some of the tribes have become quite wealthy, allowing them in turn to contribute and donate funds to the larger communities. More significantly, in the late 1980s, the Confederated Tribes of Grand Ronde, which consists of over 20 tribes and bands from western Oregon and northern California, was able to buy back more than 9,000 acres of original reservation land. This was funded in part from profits made at the Spirit Mountain Casino in Oregon, owned and operated by the Confederated Tribes of Grand Ronde. The casino, which is Oregon's number one tourist attraction, has a large hotel, live entertainment, restaurants, shops, and over 90,000 square feet of casino gaming floor.

Another example of the success of Indian gaming is represented by the Foxwoods Resort Casino in eastern Connecticut, which is owned and operated by the Mashantucket Pequot tribe. Today, the Foxwoods Resort Casino is the most profitable of all Native American gaming operations and brings in millions in profit each year. However, as recently as 1973 the tribe had only two members remaining on its impoverished reservation. In 1976, with the assistance of the Native American Rights Fund and the Indian Rights Association, the tribe managed to bring proceedings to recover former reservation land that had been sold by the state of Connecticut in 1856. Along with settling its land claims, the Pequot also began a number of economic enterprises, the most successful being the Foxwoods Resort Casino that was established in 1992. Profits from the casino have financed such things as health care and educational facilities for members of the tribe, as well as providing support for the building of the Mashantucket Pequot Museum and Research Center, which opened in 1998.

Gaming on reservations cannot provide a simple solution to the very complicated relationship between native and non-native Americans. In a telling commentary, Jim Northrup, an Ojibwe or Anishinaabeg ("Shinnob") Indian whose tribal lands are located in Minnesota, speaks about the conditions on reservations before and after the introduction of gambling on Native American land. As he notes, while bringing new forms of independence and security for some indigenous peoples, gaming has changed but not necessarily improved the persisting racial tensions in Indian-white relations.

> What was life back on the Reservations before gambling? Let's go back and take a look. In 1980 Shinnobs were facing discrimination and prejudice on a daily basis. Bigots were everywhere. The towns around the Reservation were the worst for racism. I called it a "hate circle" around the Rez.
>
> Most Americans were not aware of the problems we faced every day. Their view of us was a mix of twentieth-century Hollywood and nineteenth-century idealism. Some people were surprised that we were still here. We learned how to survive and even flourish in spite of the racism. We continued to teach our children how to live in a racist society.
>
> The system's tentacles reached deeper into our lives than those of any other population group. Once a Shinnob got wrapped up, it was difficult to escape. We were not people; we were clients, patients, or inmates. Sometimes we were lumped together and called a caseload. The probation officer talked to the judge who talked to the police who talked to the lawyer who talked to the social worker who talked to the counselor who talked to the child protection worker who talked to the probation officer. Shinnobs enmeshed in the system rarely got away without losing their dignity, their freedom, or their children.
>
> Jails always held more than their share of Shinnobs. The sentences seemed to be longer and the punishments more severe. A jury of their peers was a joke. I couldn't name one Shinnob who ever served on a jury even if you held a bayonet against my throat. . . . Going

to jail was considered normal and not an aberration. There were many family reunions held in the cell blocks. Shinnobs were 1 percent of the population of Minnesota but made up 25 percent of the jail and prison populations. It was tough being a free Indian in those days.

Shinnobs exercising their treaty rights were arrested by game wardens and harassed by white people. Wild rice, deer meat, ducks, and fish were confiscated by the game wardens. Canoes, nets, and guns were also taken away. Each arrest and confiscation was a reminder of how the United States kept its word in the treaties. People still continued to exercise their rights in spite of threats, gunfire, and bombs. They were the only ones who believed in the words of the treaties. It was hard to be a treaty believing Indian in the 1980s.

. . . We followed the Golden Rule in those days—those with the gold make the rules. Washington and foundation dollars ruled the reservations with their polices. Tribal governments were just learning to flex their economic muscles. Here it is the '90s and little has changed except the calendar. We are still facing racism, personal and institutional, every day. But there is one difference, the tribal governments have control of the gambling gold. (Northrup 1991:420–422)

Gaming on reservations is providing some Native Americans with the resources they need to fight enduring forms of discrimination and racism against indigenous peoples. At the same time, gaming profits are also providing the economic clout for some tribes to engage in mainstream political activities for the first time in this country's history. One way in which tribes have entered the political arena is by financing party campaigns and specific candidates through considerable donations. In California, such contributions have caused much concern for both Democrats and Republicans. The Agua Caliente band, which operates two highly profitable casinos in the Palm Springs area, gave more than $8 million in donations to candidates and specific causes between 1998 and 2002. These donations were the subject of a lawsuit brought against the tribe by the Fair Political Practices Commission, which prohibits such large contributions to political campaigns. According to Superior Court Judge Loren McMaster, "If large contributors to the electoral and initiative process—like the tribe—were not subject to FPPC enforcement actions the institutions and processes of California's government would be subverted . . ." (*Santa Barbara News-Press,* February 28, 2003). It is anticipated, however, that the Agua Caliente band will appeal this decision and argue that because of its tribal sovereignty it has special immunity that frees it from being bound by the state's campaign rules.

The increasing economic and political activity by Native Americans in the dominant white society has resulted in successful tribes demanding acknowledgment that not all indigenous peoples are inferior to non-Indians, operate under the same legal rules, or necessarily endorse the capitalist ideologies of Western democracies. Successful tribes and new forms of Indian capitalism are forcing white Americans to reassess their relationship to and preconceptions of Native American peoples, and along the way are helping to forge a cultural revitalization within all Native American communities, which remain the most impoverished and deprived in the United States.

Intriguingly, some Native American casino operators are turning the capitalist model of individual profit on its head by using gaming profits to support collective tribal economies and to establish museums and community centers that in many ways are revitalizing unique traditions and cultural values. This attitude conflicts with today's dominant capitalist mentality that stresses money for money's sake. The accumulation of wealth as an end in itself has been the overriding rationale for economic involvement, and it has mattered very little what one actually plans to do with one's profits. This is not to say that Native Americans casino operators are uninterested in making money. However, for many indigenous peoples, individual profit for its own sake is not the most important drive behind their entrepreneurial ventures. For many Native Americans, what matters most is the betterment of their collective social, cultural, and political condition; being able to provide adequately for future generations; and being able to participate in mainstream society while retaining their unique identities, dignity, and independence. For these Native Americans, casino gaming is simply the only avenue currently open by which they can achieve these long-term goals.

GLOBAL INDIGENOUS MOVEMENTS

Controversial issues surrounding Indian gaming are particular to contemporary U.S. society and the country's historical treatment of Native Americans. However, the issues involved share similarities with those of other indigenous movements occurring around the world in countries such as Canada, Mexico, New Zealand, and Australia. In common to all of these movements are claims to land that in turn bring economic resources and "buy" native peoples a presence in mainstream legal, political, and cultural institutions. Indigenous movements in countries other than the United States raise parallel problems for their dominant postcolonial white populations and governments that, over the past two decades, have had to take seriously and heed native peoples' rights and needs.

In Canada, aboriginal land rights claims by the Métis, First Nations, and Inuit peoples have marked the country's recent legal history. These land claims are significant because managing territory represents resources for new economic ventures such as mining, logging, industrial plants, and a wide range of activities such as shopping malls and other commercial ventures. These economic developments in turn challenge old stereotypes about native peoples that socially marginalize them as being "primitive" and "premodern."

The legal anthropologist Dara Culhane (1998) has written a wonderful account of the history of First Nations land rights claims in British Columbia in her book *The Pleasure of the Crown*. The account details the landmark case of *Delgamuukw v. Regina*, which was successful in its appeal to the Supreme Court of Canada in 1997. The case represents a benchmark in recognizing the inalienability of aboriginal land title that was deemed to exist before European contact. This recognition allowed the Supreme Court to throw out the British colonial regime's justification to claim sovereignty over First Nations' territory under the legal doctrine of *terra nullius* or "land belonging to no one." (For a discussion of this doctrine, see Chapter 2; also see Culhane 1998:37–60; Macklem 2001).

Similarly the Inuit peoples of the Arctic region, sometimes referred to outside Canada by their European name "Eskimos," have made huge advances in forcing the Canadian government to acknowledge their sovereign rights to land. Since the early 1970s, the Inuit Tapirit Kanatami (ITK) has worked primarily as a lobby organization representing the interests of the Inuit of Canada in national political circles. As a result of careful strategies and painstaking negotiations, the Canadian government formally recognized these land rights in the 1993 Nunavut Land Claims Agreement.

This agreement provides land title to the Inuit of Nunavut to 352,240 square kilometers of land in the northern part of Canada. In 1999, Nunavut became Canada's newest and largest territory (it is one-fifth the size of the entire country). The government of Nunavut now functions as a representative body dealing directly with other Canadian territories and political organizations on behalf of Inuit peoples. According to the official Web site of the ITK:

> Our cautious interest in larger scale development reshaped by land claims has now opened a new chapter of northern development. Not only have land claim agreements provided a legal and administrative framework vital to our orderly economic development, but the negotiating process has also served as a training ground for the rapid growth of Inuit expertise. Perhaps most importantly, the land claims agreements have provided significant working capital that our regional organizations can use for initiating a wide range of economic development projects that reflect local as well as regionwide ideas from an Inuit perspective. . . . Already there are new and interesting economic programs under way. Airlines, offshore and high sea fisheries, ecological and cultural tourism, Arctic foods, marine transportation, hunting and fishing for non-Inuit and real estate. These and other businesses are helping to create economic momentum which in turn helps spawn yet another level of economic spin off and, through the creation of support companies, additional employment opportunities in all sectors of the economy. (www.itk.ca/english/main/htm)

The Government of Nunavut and the economic development projects that it promotes for the betterment of all Inuit people are creating new images of Canada's indigenous peoples that conflict with romanticized and derogatory stereotypes of "Eskimos" still existing in mainstream media. Moreover, the government of Nunavut's concern is to help all Inuit people by improving educational, health care, and economic opportunities. It appears that, similar to casino enterprises on Native American reservations, Inuit capitalist ventures are not primarily about making money for money's sake but have the central goal of improving the conditions of all Inuit peoples and, in the process, preserving Inuit cultural traditions and heritage.

Parallel to what is happening in Canada, the government in Australia is being gradually forced to recognize the land claims of Australian Aborigines. This recognition acknowledges that native peoples are now political and economic players who cannot be entirely ignored or overlooked. The historic High Court *Mabo* decision in 1992 recognized the preexisting land rights of Australian Aborigines and Torres Strait Islanders to the continent prior to 1770 when Captain Cook claimed the country belonged to the British. The *Mabo* decision, like the Canadian case of *Delgamuukw,* threw out the legal fiction of *terra nullius,* permanently altering contemporary Australian law. It also paved the way for the Native Title Act of 1993, which established claims procedures for indigenous peoples (Reynolds 1996; on the *Mabo* case, see www.caa.org.au/publications/reports/MABO/implications.html).

The *Mabo* decision, the Native Title Act, and a subsequent 1996 High Court decision called *Wik* together mark legal milestones in forcing non-Aborigines to officially acknowledge Aboriginal land tenure. As argued by Rod Hagen, an anthropologist and social activist, these legal milestones

> brought Australian common law into line with the contemporary situation in other nations which had inherited the English common law system, including Canada, New Zealand, India and various former British African colonies. In this sense, *Mabo* was not a radical

decision, but a conservative one. In refusing to recognize the validity of any pre-existing indigenous rights, Australia has been the odd one out for many years. . . . Many Australians believe that the Native Title Act gave substantial new rights to Aboriginal people. This is simply not true. The indigenous rights and interests which the Native Title Act deals with derive directly from the rights and interests which indigenous peoples possessed at the time when the British Crown claimed sovereignty over the various parts of the continent. The need to deal with these rights and interests stems from the High Court's belated recognition in *Mabo* that these rights and interests received (and should always have received) protection from the common law. (www.netspace .netau/-rodhagen/nativetitle.html)

Despite the acknowledgment of Aboriginal land tenure in legislation and legal precedent, Australia's indigenous peoples are still not treated as equivalent to non-Aboriginal property-owning citizens.[1] However, although the law still does not treat all Australians as equal, limited legal reform has paved the way for some Aboriginal groups to demand a say in the political process. The image of Aborigines as politicians and advocates for land and civil rights is beginning to alter long-standing perceptions of them as "primitive," "backward," and "unsophisticated." This increasing political presence has played out in a variety of ways that are helping to improve the conditions of Australian Aboriginal peoples generally.

One arena where Aboriginal people have made a strong impact is in the development and protection of their cultural property, largely in the form of contemporary Aboriginal art. Since the 1970s the commercial market for Aboriginal art has grown enormously. The art critic Robert Hughes has described it as "the world's last great art movement." Not only are some Australian Aborigines now being recognized as artists deserving of state sponsorship and as producing art that is worthy of preservation in national museums, but increasingly local galleries that sell Aboriginal art are owned or managed by Aboriginal people. These galleries often provide sites for artist cooperatives and provide community gallery space for the display of Aboriginal works of art. By nurturing local artists, they promote Aboriginal culture, independence, and self-management. (For example, see the Web site of the Association of Northern, Kimberly and Arnhem Aboriginal Artists at www.taunet.net.au/ankaaa.) Significantly, some of the profits from art sales are given back to Aboriginal communities, most often to those clans associated with particular artists, in a concerted effort to raise the socioeconomic standards of all Aboriginal people across the country.

---

[1]For instance, under the Native Title Act, in order for a land claim to be successful, indigenous peoples must prove certain facts. They must show that (i) they have maintained a traditional connection with lands since the time of British sovereignty, and (ii) that their interests have not been "extinguished" by inconsistent acts such as a former grant of freehold title by the government. Given the historical management of Aborigines in Australia, where many indigenous peoples were wiped out by disease and massacres and remaining clans were often deliberately broken up by sending Aboriginal children far away to cities and missionary schools, these evidentiary burdens are extremely onerous. Moreover, in order for indigenous land claims to be legally acknowledged, these requirements force Aboriginal people to present themselves as "traditional," "primitive," and premodern, unconnected to contemporary urban Australian society and culture. In a profound sense, the *Mabo* decision and subsequent legal reforms operate in a discriminatory fashion, forcing Aboriginal peoples to be recognized in law only if they present themselves as different to and removed (culturally and geographically) from mainstream white Australian society and its citizens (Darian-Smith 1993; see also Povinelli 1999).

GLOBAL, NATIONAL, AND LOCAL CONNECTIONS

The examples in the previous section of indigenous land claims in Canada and Australia indicate the shift in the political and economic landscape that has occurred over the past 20 years with respect to these countries' aboriginal populations. Although legal reforms are often limited, as in the case of Australia, there is now greater awareness nationally and internationally of localized ethnic movements seeking claims to land, largely as a result of the creative use of global media, particularly the Internet. More importantly, claims of self-determination and sovereign autonomy are, in some cases, such as that of the Nunavut Inuit, creating new economic opportunities that help foster independence from centralized state agencies. These economic opportunities in turn help build new images of what it means to be an indigenous person at the start of the 21st century.

Unfortunately, the new wealth being cultivated by some indigenous peoples in the United States, and to a lesser degree in other parts of the world, is also contributing to the formation of new stereotypes about them that build on enduring prejudices and practices of discrimination. In Australia, for example, the idea of Aborigines owning land rights and participating in urban society has helped shape stereotypes among some white Australians about indigenous peoples' inability to deal with business ventures and economic independence. One result has been that the recent land rights laws of the 1990s, despite all the rhetoric of recognition and reconciliation, nonetheless continue to "contain" Aboriginal people within a narrative of their supposedly innate "primitiveness" and "backwardness." In the United States, where Indian gaming has provided a few tribes with extraordinary new levels of economic security, the stereotype of "rich Indians" looms large. Given the history of how Native Americans have been treated by the non-Indian population over the past 300 years, it is ironic that images of "rich Indians" are now being used negatively to argue for such things as cutting back on the minimal social services currently provided to what remains the poorest ethnic group in the country. Be it in the United States, Australia, or Canada, new derogatory stereotypes about native peoples are emerging at precisely the same moment that these people are participating in significant ways in mainstream social and political arenas for the first time. These new stereotypes indicate the widespread insecurity about treating indigenous peoples as social, legal, and political equals.

In December 2002, *Time* magazine published two feature articles on Indian gaming that reinforced a derogatory stereotype about "rich" Native Americans. These articles played on popular stories about Native Americans that have been discussed throughout this case study, such as the myths that Native Americans do not pay taxes, do not abide by U.S. law, ignore local non-Indian community interests, and function without regulatory oversight of their gaming practices. The articles were soundly condemned by the National Indian Gaming Association, whose chair, Ernie Stevens, Jr., sent a public letter to *Time* magazine stating that "we can hardly believe that an organization led by Ted Turner can, without blushing, publish stories suggesting that others should not pursue economic ventures in America" (see www.pechanga.net). The American Gaming Association (AGA) also disapproved of the *Time* articles, declaring in a position statement:

While the American Gaming Association does not take a position on Indian gaming, we do take issue with any attempts by the media to distort the facts about legal gaming in America. The recent *Time* magazine articles on Indian gaming are just the latest examples of how innuendo has taken the place of factual reporting when it involves the gaming industry. . . . The AGA may not agree with the tribes on every issue, but we do agree that *Time* magazine's article did not accurately reflect the full scope of benefits casino gaming has brought to many of our communities. (see www.pechanga.net)

Despite the negative images about Native Americans presented in popular media such as *Time* magazine, in real terms a few Native Americans are making positive socioeconomic advancements and, in the process, slowly altering how some white Americans think about them. Certainly tribal casinos are by no means the final answer to enduring postcolonial images of, and prejudice against, the poorest minority in the United States. We all have a long way to go before true social, political, and economic equality can be achieved. Still, with all of its problems, and in the context of governmental neglect and a general denial of social responsibility, gaming on reservations provides one avenue for some tribes to empower themselves and begin to ameliorate the gross inequities that are a legacy of centuries of injustice and discrimination.

Appendix A
Answers to Common Questions about Indian Gaming[1]

Q. Did the Indian Gaming Regulatory Act 1988 (IGRA) create Indian gaming?

A. No. Gaming is a right of Indian nations. Large-scale Indian gaming, mainly in the form of bingo, predated IGRA by about 10 years. The U.S. Supreme Court in 1987 recognized Indian people's right to run gaming when it ruled that states have no authority to regulate gaming on Indian land if such gaming is permitted outside the reservation for any other purpose (*California v. Cabazon*). Congress established the legal basis for this right when it passed the IGRA in 1988.

Q. How many tribes have signed compacts with the state of California?

A. By September 10, 1999, 58 tribal governments had signed tribal-state compacts with Governor Gray Davis. After that time, three additional tribes signed tribal-state gaming compacts, bringing the total number of compacts in California to 61. The compacts were signed by Secretary of the Interior Bruce Babbitt and were printed in the *Federal Register* on May 16, 2000.

Q. Will nongaming tribes benefit from Indian gaming?

A. Yes. For the first time in U.S. history, the compacts negotiated between the California tribal governments and the state of California included a provision for revenue sharing with nongaming tribes.

Q. How do tribes use the revenue generated from Indian gaming?

A. Gaming on Indian reservations is operated by tribes to fund governmental programs. The IGRA requires that all revenues from tribal gaming operations be used solely for governmental or charitable purposes. In much the same way as state governments determine the use of lottery revenues, tribal governments determine how gaming proceeds are to be spent. Indian tribes are using gaming revenue to build houses, schools, roads, and sewer and water systems; to fund health care and education for their people; and to develop a strong, diverse economic base for the future.

Q. Are Indians required to pay taxes?

A. Yes. All Indian people pay federal income, FICA, and social security taxes. Only the small percentage of Indians who live and work on their own federally recognized reservations—not unlike soldiers and their families living on military installations—are exempt from paying state income and property taxes. However, they still pay sales taxes and all other special and excise taxes. Indian

[1]These questions and answers appear on the California Nations Indian Gaming Association Web page (www.cniga.com). Reprinted with permission of the CNIGA.

gaming is now a $10.6 billion industry that creates jobs, increases economic activity, and generates tax revenue both on and off the reservation. Consider the following: In San Diego County alone, tribal gaming has been responsible for the creation of more than 5,000 well-paying jobs, with a payroll of $44 million per year (and the associated payroll taxes and employee income taxes).

Q. Who supports Indian gaming?

A. A majority of Americans support Indian gaming. Public opinion surveys both nationally and within various states have conclusively demonstrated that the public strongly supports gaming on Indian reservations. In the 1998 elections, 13 state and local referendums that dealt with gaming and Indian gaming were passed because of overwhelming support from people in all walks of life. In 1998 California voters passed Proposition 5 with more than 63 percent voter approval. The following year Proposition 1A was passed with 64 percent of the votes.

Q. How is Indian gaming regulated?

A. The tribes, as governments, are the first to be vigilant in protecting the integrity of projects they rely upon to feed, clothe, educate, and employ their people. Tribal governmental gaming is regulated on three separate and distinct levels, in contrast to the single level of commercial gaming regulation. The first level is the tribes themselves; the Indian Gaming Regulatory Act (IGRA) mandates tribes to establish a regulatory body (tribal regulators and commissions) to keep operations in compliance with local ordinances and state compacts. The second level is the State Gaming Department, which regulates the areas that have been negotiated with the tribes in tribal-state compacts. The third level is the National Indian Gaming Commission, which became operable in February 1993 to oversee the regulation of Indian gaming. Other oversight entities include the federal government, the Department of Justice, the Federal Bureau of Investigation (FBI), and the Bureau of Indian Affairs.

Q. Does Indian gaming work as a means of economic development for tribes and states?

A. Yes. Indian gaming is providing substantial economic benefits in states where the tribes and states have worked together to develop mutual goals. The IGRA is working to the benefit of Indians and non-Indians in several states, including California, Washington, Arizona, Minnesota, Wisconsin, Michigan, and Connecticut. Reservations are slowly recovering from decades of well-meaning but failed governmental programs. Indians and non-Indians alike are proudly leaving welfare rolls and getting payroll checks; they are now taxpayers instead of tax users. Local and state governments are enjoying increased tax revenues. Only in those few instances where states have failed to negotiate fair compacts in "good faith" in violation of IGRA has the process not worked.

Q. Are better economic development alternatives to gaming available to tribes?

A. Indian gaming has been the first, and only, economic development tool available on reservations. Most reservations are in remote places on inconveniently located or useless land that nobody else wanted. Before tribal government gaming, public and private sector economic development efforts on reservations had little success. So far states have not proposed any specific or credible alternatives to Indian gaming as a meaningful source of tribal revenues and jobs. The National